Leeza Gibbons
Scrapbooking Traditions

Meredith® Books

Des Moines, Iowa

WRITTEN AND PRODUCED BY: Leeza Gibbons
EDITOR: Christine Hofmann-Bourque
DESIGNER: Sue Ellibee
COVER PHOTOGRAPHER: Edmund Barr
PHOTOSTYLING ASSISTANT: Robin Tucker
HAIRSTYLIST AND MAKEUP ARTIST FOR LEEZA GIBBONS: Katharine Kremp
WARDROBE FOR LEEZA GIBBONS: Julie Kozak

Published by Meredith® Books, Des Moines, Iowa.

acknowledgments

One of my mother's enduring gifts was awakening me to the power of memories and the blessing of legacies. Thank you, Mom, for encouraging me to tell my story and now yours.

Thanks to my family, whose inspiration is abundant and whose forgiveness is limitless. I adored every minute spent pouring over photos of you while deciding which ones to use in this book. To my husband, Steve, your approval was like the sweetest kiss. To my children, Lexi, Troy, and Nathan—you are the greatest blessings in my life. Even though you are growing faster every second, my scrapbook pages keep you deliciously frozen in time.

To my girlfriends, who always believe in me, thanks for being there yet again. Thanks especially to Holly Tyrer, who (as only a true friend would) told me when my scrapbooking pages weren't cut straight, my measurements weren't aligned, and my photographs weren't printed well—and then went on to help me make it all better. To Vincent Arcuri, thank you for reminding me to laugh at myself. There will be no more voicemail messages at 3 a.m.! On this project and so many others, your support has meant the world. I'm grateful to my friend and confidant John Hunter. Thanks for always helping me find the right words. And to Cheri Ingram, thanks for igniting my creativity and reminding me that I am enough.

Thank you to the guest artists in this book, scrapbookers Lori Bergmann, Nicole Gartland, Tracy Kyle, and Erin Terrell. You are all so talented and added such class to our efforts. You even managed to use my scrapbooking products, Leeza Gibbons Legacies, in ways I'd never thought of before! I loved it all. Thanks so much to my partners at Xyron for their support and belief in me. Tobianne Hall, Kathleen George, Amy Romano, and Nadine Dekema—you were wonderful. Thank you for pushing this effort forward with such passion. And to Mel Berger, Rick Bradley, and Scott Zolke—every girl should be as lucky to have three men as cool as you in her corner! Thanks.

Finally, to Terry Sutton, whose exquisite taste and business acumen guided me to this path: We are only getting started. I'm glad you are there to lead the way.

table of contents

WHEN IN DOUBT, HUG

Nathan in a BOX

Tell me about your life

Maybe it's because my mom is losing her memories that I have become almost obsessed with preserving mine. After Mom was diagnosed with Alzheimer's disease, I found myself digging through boxes of old photographs. The one that haunts me most is a black-and-white picture of Mom at age 17, sitting with my dad in a little boat on a calm lake. She seemed to be trying so hard to look mature and sophisticated, yet I could sense the girl underneath who had never left her small town of Summerton, South Carolina, until she met Daddy. I want so much to ask my mother whether she was nervous about her life ahead. Was she excited about "keeping house"? I wish that I had spent time—before Alzheimer's came into our lives—mining her memory for those little recollections that would be so comforting now. That's part of the reason I record my own feelings and thoughts for my children.

Simply put, memories matter. That's why I love scrapbooking. It preserves our life stories and moments on paper. Scrapbooks reflect how we spend our time, who we love, where we visit. Collectively, those things reveal what I call our unique "soulprint" on the planet. When others look at our books, they get an intimate view of who we are. When we reflect on our moments of joy and celebration, as well as drama and turmoil, we can see our own soulprint come alive. Scrapbooks give us a tangible way to read our own life stories, even while we're writing the current chapter.

Why am I writing this book? To encourage you to tell your life story—and to do it in a new and meaningful way. Scrapbooks are a wonderful way to ensure that your memories survive as a legacy for the next generations.

Now, I'm not a scrapbooking maven by any stretch of the imagination. In fact, those who know me best would say I'm not "crafty" at all, and my first scrapbooks often took on the look of a third-grade project gone bad. But I'm hooked. I started scrapbooking seriously six years ago, between

.

nighttime feedings of my youngest son, Nathan. What I created back then was mostly a glorified photo album with a few stickers added to the pages. But those were important first attempts at preserving my memories.

If you've never put together a scrapbook before, it can seem overwhelming. Relax. I created many of the scrapbook pages in this book while sitting at my dining room table surrounded by stacks of paper, boxes of photos, and spools of ribbon. If I can do it, so can anyone with paper and scissors. My scrapbooking philosophy is straightforward: Keep it simple. All the pages in this book were created with easy techniques—mostly cutting and taping—that guarantee success.

After you explore this book, I'm certain that you'll feel secure in your ability to create a scrapbook and that you'll appreciate the many reasons for doing it. At the core of each scrapbook page is love. That's it. Love for the person featured, love for the moment in time being preserved, love for the values and traditions that are reflected in the story of your life.

So here's the deal. As women, we work through issues by talking. It's how we relieve stress and make sense of our world. So I've structured this book as a conversation between us. I'll prompt you to "tell me about" certain things in your life. And to get you going, I'll share some of the moments that have made their way into my scrapbooks. But I want your scrapbook to be as unique as your laughter (something good to write about) and as original as your special macaroni-and-cheese recipe (a great addition to a page). Tell your stories in your own way. You have sole custody of your life; make sure you are on the record with it.

If you are a beginner scrapbooker, welcome to a pastime that honors who you are, where you came from, and what your dreams and values are. If you are a veteran, thanks for paving a path filled with such creativity and soul-satisfying expression. Enjoy *Scrapbooking Traditions*!

The Leeza Gibbons Memory Foundation

I was in sixth grade when my mother, Gloria Jean Gibbons, helped me identify my talent for storytelling. At that moment, I knew my career would involve bringing other people's stories to life. Now I've been entrusted to tell my most important and personal story, about the challenges my family faces from the cruel, unrelenting enemy known as Alzheimer's disease. We lost my grandmother to Alzheimer's, and we lose a little more of my mom to it each day.

"Promise me that you'll use what is happening to us," my mother said to me after she was diagnosed. "Make it count." She wanted to be an advocate, not a victim. I began to fulfill that promise in 2002 when I formed The Leeza Gibbons Memory Foundation. It offers comfort and care both to those suffering from any memory disorder—such as those caused by Alzheimer's, Parkinson's, multiple sclerosis, and brain trauma—and to their caregivers.

One way we do that is through Leeza's Place, an intimate setting where families can gain education, empowerment, and energy as they prepare for the journey ahead. It's a place to find a web of support and to learn about the latest treatments, preventions, and experimental studies. A variety of programs—including scrapbooking sessions—help families create an archive of treasured memories before they are lost. There are currently two Leeza's Place locations, in New York City and West Melbourne, Florida. Openings in New Orleans and in Joliet, Illinois, and are planned for 2005.

We believe there is life after diagnosis. We are passionately committed to offering comfort and care while we work on a realistic strategy for finding a cure. All services are free and are offered with the belief that families dealing with any memory disorder deserve guidance and support. For more information, please visit www.leezasplace.org.

Tell me about …
your heritage

"Who am I?" We spend our entire lives trying to answer that fundamental question. I believe many of the real insights lie in the past. There's so much to be learned from the triumphs and struggles of your grandparents, your great-aunts and -uncles, your parents—all those people who paved the way for you. Entire generations have their courses set by those who came before, often without any real knowledge or appreciation of how it happened. That's why a good place to start scrapbooking is with a page about your heritage.

My Grandfather Dyson died when my mom, Gloria Jean, was 12 years old. But I grew up hearing stories of Granddaddy's kindness and generosity and how he taught my mom, whom he nicknamed "Jeepers," to drive a tractor. Mostly I loved Mom's stories of how Granddaddy came to her in a dream before the birth of each of her three children. In the dream he would say, "Jeepers, you're having a little girl (or boy), and the baby's just fine." Mom says she never worried about childbirth, and she knew she would have one boy and two girls. I used to ask my mother, "If you die before me, will you find a way—like Granddaddy—to come to me in my dreams?" She said, "Yes," that dreams would be the way we would communicate when earthbound words were no longer ours. Mom has been long lost behind the fog of Alzheimer's disease, but she was right: Like her father did with her, she speaks to me in my dreams. It's important to me that my children know this piece of who their great-grandfather and grandmother were—because it's also a part of who I am and who they are. It's a story perfectly suited for my scrapbook pages.

If you're lucky enough to have your grandparents and parents still with you, make sure you take photographs that capture them in the unguarded moments that reveal their personalities. I love this picture of me with my dad, Carlos, and my mom, Jean. Don't get me wrong, those posed photos from family reunions are valuable too. But it's much more fun to create a scrapbook page about your father's joke-telling ability, for instance, if you have the photos to match.

ALL THAT WE LOVE DEEPLY
BECOMES A PART OF US.
❯ HELEN KELLER ❮

I'm asking you to think of yourself as a family documentarian. Your medium will be your scrapbook. Share stories about your relatives' personality quirks, their religious practices, where they lived, the dishes that always ended up on their dinner tables, the countries they emigrated from, and the people they fell madly in love with. Your written words—what scrapbookers call journaling—will give old photos context and speak to future generations. If you can, write about the emotions behind the pictures and events. Filled with these intimate details, your scrapbook will preserve the powerful stories missing from many family trees.

Now, I have a lifelong addiction to self-help books. Hours of reading in the bathtub have convinced me of their therapeutic value. They're right up there with a call to a good friend or a pint of ice cream. Regardless of the author or the philosophical vantage point, they all say that getting

LOVE. My scrapbooking motto is "Less is more." This page (ABOVE LEFT) of me and my husband, Steve, accompanies the story of how we met. The layout is basic: One photo with one little word says it all. My parents' love affair is a perfect topic for this heritage page (ABOVE RIGHT). The no-fuss design not only has the clean, classic look I love but also suits my somewhat limited crafting skills, which include cutting, gluing, and taping.

CARLOS AND JEAN. When I enlarge old photos for which I don't have negatives, the images can be grainy. That doesn't bother me. It's the smiles in the photos that matter, not perfect quality.

Fifty years of marriage began with a soldier boy and his 17-year-old fiancée, my Mom and Dad, posing for pictures in a rowboat. My mother had dreams much bigger than the small town from which she came. Daddy promised he would help make them all come true. This graduation day kiss shows the first of three degrees they earned together. His name is on the diploma but it was a partnership all the way.

Dad's Sense of Humor

We used to call my Dad "Dr. G." He is, in fact, a Ph.D., but for all his scholarly background, it is his joke telling that I think is his most memorable characteristic. Mom used to roll her eyes in horror as he would wind up at family gatherings. I loved it and would often join in—to the utter shock of my siblings. It's the bond that Daddy and I shared for as long as I could remember.

The jokes weren't really that funny. What was hysterical was the way Dad would tell them. His ramblings were so well known that crowds would gather as if they were watching a theatrical performance. Dad always kept a joke file and anytime he heard something good, he would make a note of it. But we liked the classics—the ones he told at every dinner party. I learned from my Dad that a sense of humor was a powerful shield against a world that often takes itself too seriously. Laughter works with all people from all cultures. If I ever got sad, Dad would say, "Tell a few jokes, honey, and call me in the morning."

started—whether it's on weight loss or learning to speak a foreign language—is the most important step. That's so true, isn't it? It's the same with scrapbooking. Once you get started, ideas will flow. I begin by identifying the pictures and stories I want to use. Then I find the papers that will complement them. I like to lay out lots of possibilities—photo corners, ribbons, frames—and play. There are no rules! Some scrapbookers have a plan; I usually don't. Do what's fun for you. This shouldn't be a chore.

"Gourmet means more gravy or cheese."

My roots are deeply planted in the South. I'm a yes-ma'am-sayin', sweet-iced-tea-drinkin', boiled-peanut-eatin' kind of girl who loves grits, magnolias and pine trees. Even though my Southern accent may have left me, the images and memories of growing up in South Carolina never have.
For us, Sunday dinner was always a carbohydrate-loading, artery-clogging extravaganza. Gourmet simply meant add more gravy or cheese. I remember seeing my Mom in the kitchen opening boxes and cans and dumping it all together into a casserole dish to be topped with Ritz crackers or french-fried onions. If you added enough topping you could "cover a multitude of culinary sins," she would say. It always tasted good to me, but it was usually cold by the time Daddy got through blessing the food!

Case in point: my scrapbook page (RIGHT) about my roots, which are deeply planted in the South.

I'm a yes-ma'am-sayin', sweet-iced-tea-drinkin', boiled-peanut-eatin' kind of girl who loves grits, magnolias, and pine trees. Even though my Southern accent has left me, my memories of growing up in South Carolina haven't. At our house, Sunday dinner was a carbohydrate-loaded, artery-clogging extravaganza. "Gourmet" meant extra gravy or cheese. My mom believed that adding enough toppings to a casserole (Ritz crackers and french-fried onions were her favorites) could "cover a multitude of culinary sins." Now that my mom's memories have been lost to Alzheimer's, I feel compelled to tell her stories—and share her cooking secrets—with my children, who have known her only as a sad, vacant woman who doesn't speak. I treasure these old snapshots of my mom smiling in the kitchen and at the table with me and my sister, Cammy. By capturing my memories on paper, I can be sure they will live on, long past the storyteller. In the end, I think that's one way we get to live forever.

Why didn't the hot dog star in the movies? over →

P U L L

DAD'S SENSE OF HUMOR. What a riot! That's me with my dad, Carlos (OPPOSITE), in 1959 and 1979. To include a hidden joke, adhere a piece of card stock to the underside of a metal-rim tag, write your joke on the paper, and embellish the tag with the word "pull" and a ribbon handle. Next to the main photo, cut a vertical slit that is slightly larger than the width of the paper joke. Slide the joke through the page. To protect the joke from damage, cover it on the back of the page with a large square of paper, adhering only around the edges.

My Grandparents:
Dr. Yuan Kai & Wei Yung Grace Huang
Bangkok, Thailand
Summer of 1955

MORE INSPIRATION Simple but stunning, this single-photo GRANDPARENTS layout keeps the spotlight where it should be: on the vintage black-and-white photo of the scrapbooker's Thai grandparents. When creating pages about your relatives, be sure to identify them by their full names at least once. You may know exactly who "Uncle Joe" is, but chances are, in 100 years your great-great-great-grandchildren will need more details. When working with embellishments, be creative. The graphic design on the back of a brown-and-red ribbon best suited this page, so it's glued on wrong side up.

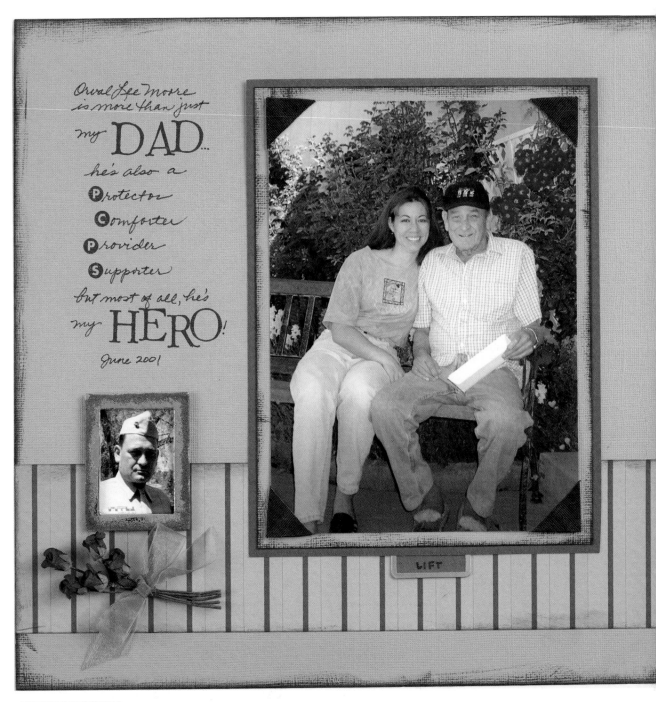

Orval Lee Moore
is more than just

my DAD...

he's also a

Ⓟrotector

Ⓒomforter

Ⓟrovider

Ⓢupporter

but most of all, he's

my HERO!

June 2001

LIFT

MORE INSPIRATION A short-but-sweet list of the things this scrapbooker loves about her dad on DAD IS MY HERO proves that journaling can take whatever form you want: a list, a caption, a long story, a name with a date. Let your personality shine through by combining stamped letters with handwriting. Notice that this handwriting isn't exactly straight, but that adds to the charm. For an aged effect, the edges of some of these papers were rubbed with brown ink and a stamp pad before they were applied to the page. For details on the hidden journaling (denoted by the "lift" tag), see page 42.

Lovebirds

Ray Bergmann
(age 24)
and
Dora Hammer
(age 18.5)

1945

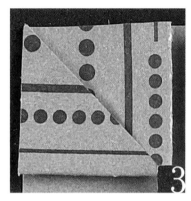

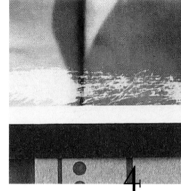

BEST DISTRESSED PAGES. Stretch your creative muscles with these simple techniques that lend an aged feel perfect for heritage pages. (1) Distressed background paper: Transform plain white card stock using stamp pads and inks in at least three colors (this example uses browns and reds). Apply the ink directly to the paper by rubbing the stamp pads in a random, swirly motion, one color at a time, until you achieve the desired effect. While the ink is still wet, use a large stipple brush to soften the lines in places. (2) Distressed frame: Paint a silver-tone frame with cranberry red acrylic paint. While the paint is still slightly wet, apply a brown antique glaze over top. The red paint will come off in random places for a terrific mottled effect. (3) Pleated photo mat: Just cut and fold! Cut 1" wide strips of patterned paper and score them at 1", $\frac{1}{4}$", and $\frac{3}{4}$" intervals in a repeating pattern. Fold along the score lines, first to the right and then to the left, to get the pleated effect. Glue the strips just inside a large photo mat and miter the corners if desired. (4) Distressed photo: To give the edges of a photograph a well-worn look, copy the original vintage photo onto photo paper, then use sandpaper to gently rub the perimeter.

MORE INSPIRATION   Admit it: You have boxes of vintage family photos, like the ones on this LOVEBIRDS page (OPPOSITE), gathering dust in the cellar—and no clue who the people are. There's an easy remedy. At the next family get-together, pass the pictures around to uncover the missing names and stories. Use special wax-based, photo-safe pencils to write names and dates on the backs of photos; the soft points won't damage photos the way lead can.

Leeza's idea starters

It's up to you to make certain that your family legacy lives on. Jump-start the brainstorming for your heritage pages by asking yourself these questions.

(1) What are your parents' full names? Your grandparents' full names? How did they meet and fall in love? What were their religions? Where were they born?

(2) Were you named for anyone in your family? If not, where did your name come from?

(3) Where did you grow up? What regional distinctions did you pick up? A deep Southern drawl? A love for New England lobster rolls?

(4) Which "characters" in your family always provide the drama? How would you describe them?

(5) Who most influenced your personality? For example, did you inherit your grandmother's passion for cats? Or your mother's love of flea markets?

(6) Do you have any old letters packed away in boxes? They can be a great source for heritage information and details. They are also valuable items to include on scrapbook pages.

(7) What did your ancestors do for a living? What kind of houses did they live in? Do you remember visiting any of them?

(8) What world events influenced your parents or grandparents? If they're alive, ask them to describe the impact. Use a voice recorder so no detail is lost.

On the paper trail

Decorative papers are the foundation of every scrapbook page, so have a blast stocking up on pretty papers in subtle stripes, perky polka dots, groovy graphics, and more. Pick the right papers with these tips.

WEIGHTY ISSUES. The most common scrapbooking paper is card stock, a colored paper that's heavier and stiffer than the kind typically used for printing on your home computer. Card stock gives your pages body and doesn't bend or wrinkle when you're working with it. Use it to build backgrounds, mat photos, create borders, make journaling boxes, and more.

ALL THE OPTIONS. There are as many paper choices as there are color choices. Mix card stock with patterned papers and vellum, a lighter-weight translucent paper that can be used for journaling or to add a soft touch over a photo. Lined papers make journaling foolproof. Simply write what you want, then cut the paper to the desired size and shape. Ink-jet papers are safe to run through your home computer printer and can be used to print journaling entries.

SIZE MATTERS. Most scrapbooking papers are sold in 8½"×11" or 12"×12" sizes, though you can also buy smaller sizes, such as 6"×6". You'll use large, uncut papers as the basis for your pages, then cut up other papers to mat your photos and make page borders, punched designs, and other trims. All the scrapbook pages in this book are a generous 12"×12", a size that fits perfectly in a 12"×12" album. Remember: The bigger the page, the more room you'll have to be creative with photographs, embellishments, and journaling.

QUALITY COUNTS. Always choose scrapbook papers that are acid-free and lignin-free (lignin is a substance produced in plants; it occurs in paper naturally). These will be archival-quality and won't damage the photographs, journaling, and embellishments you place on the page. The paper also should be buffered, which means it was treated with an alkaline substance to prevent acidity.

Tell me about...
your family traditions

I cooked up our Thanksgiving Day Gratitude Hike a few years ago after an obscenely large dinner of turkey and dressing and homemade pies. Everyone was lying around in a post-dinner daze, watching football on TV. I didn't like the sports-induced trance that was threatening to kidnap my husband and kids, so I decided to crank up the activity level.

"This will be great, gang!" I said. "We'll all write down what we're thankful for, hike up to the top of the canyon, and read our thoughts to each other! It's a way to embrace the true meaning of Thanksgiving!" Groans from all. Only Crystal, my yellow Lab, seemed even remotely interested. But those in our house have learned that once Mom gets "the look," only complicity in the passion du jour will make it go away. Soon, my husband, Steve, and my children Lexi and Troy were writing their lists. (Nathan, my youngest, hadn't come along yet.) Shortly thereafter, we trudged onward and upward through the canyon.

It was a gorgeous day, and the top of the hill was calm and deserted. As we sat in a circle and read our lists out loud, something happened. The hike, the spectacular setting, and the simplicity of our statements made gratitude more real for us.

Over the years, our lists have evolved along with the authors. Some of us compose for weeks prior to Thanksgiving. Others dash off something the morning of. A few years ago, we added to the tradition with plastic champagne glasses of apple cider for the kids and the good stuff for Steve and me. I invariably cry and struggle with the camera so we can capture the moment before the sun sets—and so I can have photos for my scrapbook pages.

Most families are blessed with more traditions than they might realize. Our family—that's me with my children (FROM LEFT), Lexi, 15; Troy, 13; and Nate, 7—is no different. Every year we listen to the same music when we decorate the holiday tree, and the kids make the same jokes about my dry-as-a-bone Thanksgiving turkey. Such events become meaningful when we assign value to them, and scrapbooking is one way to do just that.

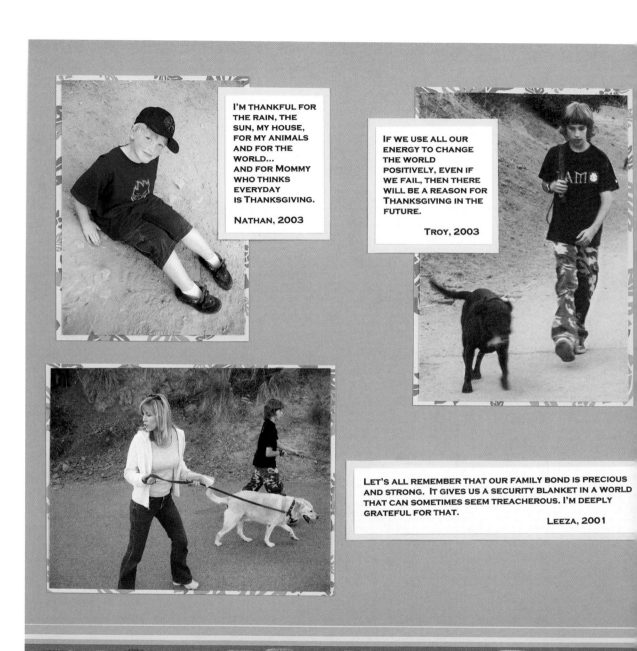

I'M THANKFUL FOR THE RAIN, THE SUN, MY HOUSE, FOR MY ANIMALS AND FOR THE WORLD... AND FOR MOMMY WHO THINKS EVERYDAY IS THANKSGIVING.

NATHAN, 2003

IF WE USE ALL OUR ENERGY TO CHANGE THE WORLD POSITIVELY, EVEN IF WE FAIL, THEN THERE WILL BE A REASON FOR THANKSGIVING IN THE FUTURE.

TROY, 2003

LET'S ALL REMEMBER THAT OUR FAMILY BOND IS PRECIOUS AND STRONG. IT GIVES US A SECURITY BLANKET IN A WORLD THAT CAN SOMETIMES SEEM TREACHEROUS. I'M DEEPLY GRATEFUL FOR THAT.

LEEZA, 2001

our thanksgiving

GRATITUDE HIKE. Don't get hung up on matching a holiday to its traditional colors. Though it may seem logical to use rich fall colors for Thanksgiving pages, I did these pages in purples and pale yellows, and they look beautiful. To go with the photos, I typed up excerpts from my family's letters. Because our dog Crystal couldn't tell us her thoughts, I included her paw print on the page. (I dipped her paw in ink while she was asleep!) I firmly believe perfection is overrated: Though I always proofread my journaling before it's final, sometimes a spelling mistake (or two) will slip by me.

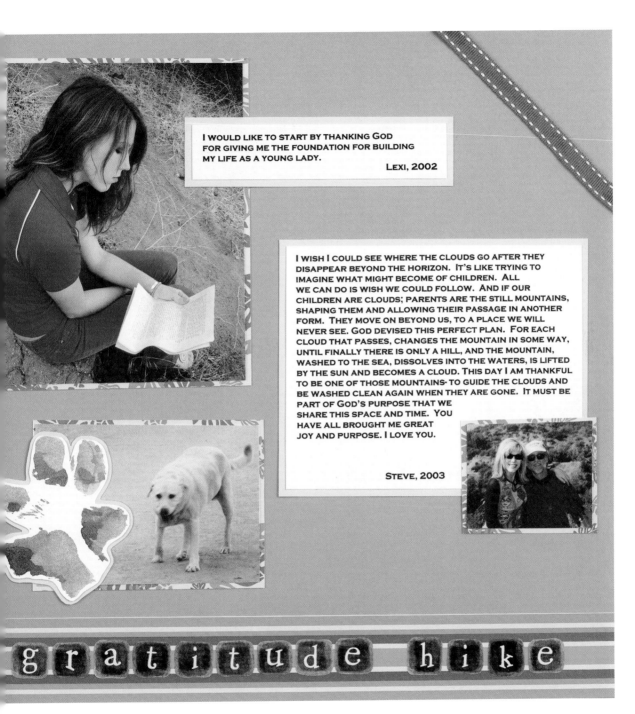

I WOULD LIKE TO START BY THANKING GOD FOR GIVING ME THE FOUNDATION FOR BUILDING MY LIFE AS A YOUNG LADY.

LEXI, 2002

I WISH I COULD SEE WHERE THE CLOUDS GO AFTER THEY DISAPPEAR BEYOND THE HORIZON. IT'S LIKE TRYING TO IMAGINE WHAT MIGHT BECOME OF CHILDREN. ALL WE CAN DO IS WISH WE COULD FOLLOW. AND IF OUR CHILDREN ARE CLOUDS; PARENTS ARE THE STILL MOUNTAINS, SHAPING THEM AND ALLOWING THEIR PASSAGE IN ANOTHER FORM. THEY MOVE ON BEYOND US, TO A PLACE WE WILL NEVER SEE. GOD DEVISED THIS PERFECT PLAN. FOR EACH CLOUD THAT PASSES, CHANGES THE MOUNTAIN IN SOME WAY, UNTIL FINALLY THERE IS ONLY A HILL, AND THE MOUNTAIN, WASHED TO THE SEA, DISSOLVES INTO THE WATERS, IS LIFTED BY THE SUN AND BECOMES A CLOUD. THIS DAY I AM THANKFUL TO BE ONE OF THOSE MOUNTAINS- TO GUIDE THE CLOUDS AND BE WASHED CLEAN AGAIN WHEN THEY ARE GONE. IT MUST BE PART OF GOD'S PURPOSE THAT WE SHARE THIS SPACE AND TIME. YOU HAVE ALL BROUGHT ME GREAT JOY AND PURPOSE. I LOVE YOU.

STEVE, 2003

gratitude hike

Prayers & Rainbows

There is something especially important about a ritual at night, when the goblins of youth and head-churning pressures of adulthood creep around under the bed—and when we need some reassuring comfort. For my family, the nightly constant is the saying of prayers and the singing of something sentimental and—some would say—sappy. "The Rainbow Connection" is one of my favorites.

My favorite lyrics are,
"What's so amazing that keeps us stargazing
And what do we think we might see?
Someday we'll find it, the rainbow connection
The lovers, the dreamers, and me."

It's a wonderful song about the mysteries of life and the wonderment of it all. I've used it to launch lots of discussions about things we can't see, but we feel in our heart. Things we can't prove, but we know to be true. Discussions about faith. I don't imagine my children will remember "The Rainbow Connection" because of my, well, less-than-Streisand-esque delivery of the tune, but I suspect that memory will help them through a tough adult night. They may not remember every specific childhood prayer we said, but I hope when they're all grown-up that they'll continue to cap their days with quiet minutes of divine communication.

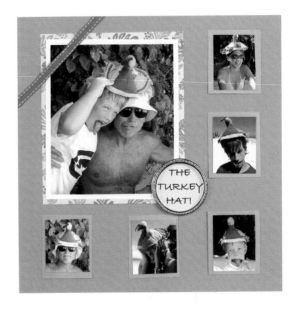

What are your family traditions? Don't be put off by the formal feeling of the word "traditions." Do you always sing the same song in the car on road trips? When your mother visits, do you cook the same dish? Are there marks on a wall in the bedroom chronicling the kids' growth? All of these things, big and small, are traditions. They are the backbone of our lives. They should be in your scrapbook because the more we are aware of our traditions, the more we can value them.

One of our small traditions involves a turkey hat (ABOVE). One Thanksgiving I made a casserole that I served covered with a tacky fabric turkey hat, which I bought at the grocery store. (My colorful presentations make up for my lack of culinary talent!) I decided to make everyone at the table take turns wearing the hat. Years passed, and the hat became a Thanksgiving constant. Two Novembers ago, we were in Thailand. Needless to say, the lovely Thai people don't celebrate our American holiday, so we had a picnic on the beach. I forgot my sunscreen, the kids' swim goggles, and a converter for my curling iron, but I remembered to pack the turkey hat. The old bird is getting tattered, but I plan to pass it down to my kids along with their christening gown and baby blankies.

Now you may find, as I do, that your scrapbooking style follows your moods. Sometimes I'm neutral and classic, and other times I feel more whimsical and colorful. But almost always, I need to keep my designs—and the techniques I use—simple. That is one of the reasons I created Leeza Gibbons Legacies, my scrapbooking line of color-coordinated papers, albums, and tools. When I started scrapbooking, I used to stand in the crafts store feeling overwhelmed by the volume of tools and gadgets. I wanted to

PRAYERS & RAINBOWS. This layout (OPPOSITE) is super-simple. The photo of Nate, Lexi, and Troy was scanned into the computer and printed directly onto yellow card stock, along with my journaling. (When printing directly onto background paper, practice using inexpensive plain white paper to ensure the text placement is correct.) Striped paper cut into strips was adhered to the card stock to make a simple border. The title was printed on plain purple paper and glued on top.

simplify that process and give scrapbookers like me the peace of mind that comes from a straight-forward approach to design. You can certainly find techniques and tools in the scrapbooking world to challenge the most advanced mechanical engineer, but those aren't for me.

Take a look at the pages in this book. They didn't take a lot of time to make, but because they incorporate beautiful papers and embellishments, they look like real treasures.

BOX IT UP. Incorporate hidden journaling (it's underneath the title, OPPOSITE) as you replicate this boxy layout. (1) Glue two precut 6"×6" squares to a 12"×12" patterned paper to create the color-block background. (2) Convert four color photos to black and white, and mat them on contrasting solid-color paper. (3) Print the journaling on the back (white) side of a solid-color paper, then cut the paper and fold it in half to create the hidden text box. (4) Print the page title on a contrasting solid-color paper; cut it into a square and adhere it to the top of the journaling card. (5) Embellish the title square with a dot-and-dash border, hand-drawn with a fine-point pen.

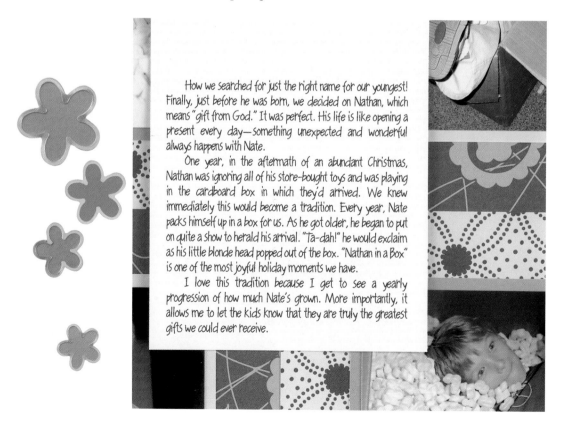

How we searched for just the right name for our youngest! Finally, just before he was born, we decided on Nathan, which means "gift from God." It was perfect. His life is like opening a present every day—something unexpected and wonderful always happens with Nate.

One year, in the aftermath of an abundant Christmas, Nathan was ignoring all of his store-bought toys and was playing in the cardboard box in which they'd arrived. We knew immediately this would become a tradition. Every year, Nate packs himself up in a box for us. As he got older, he began to put on quite a show to herald his arrival. "Ta-dah!" he would exclaim as his little blonde head popped out of the box. "Nathan in a Box" is one of the most joyful holiday moments we have.

I love this tradition because I get to see a yearly progression of how much Nate's grown. More importantly, it allows me to let the kids know that they are truly the greatest gifts we could ever receive.

NATHAN IN A BOX. These are among my most joyful Christmas moments. Every year Nate packs himself up as a gift to me, and this page captures the spirit of the occasion perfectly. I love how the color-block design plays up the "box" theme.

Nathan in a BOX

Every year since Tristan was born, we have purchased a new snow globe for Christmas. We go to many stores before we find the one that we decide to purchase. The snow globes have become an important part of our holiday season, from purchasing one, unpacking them all and admiring them around our home. Yes, I know that we are going to end up with a lot of snow globes, in fact, probably way more than one family needs. But it just would not be Christmas without a new snow globe!

ChRisTmas TraDitiOn # 4

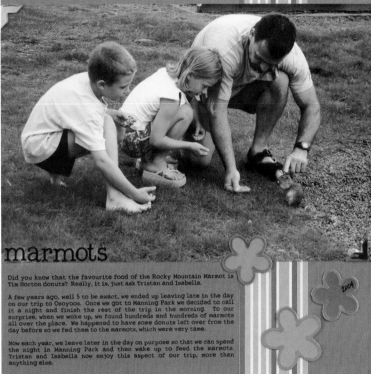

things in the garden...

Kyle family tradition

grandparent's garden, my parents, and mine

marmots

Did you know that the favourite food of the Rocky Mountain Marmot is Tim Horton donuts? Really, it is, just ask Tristan and Isabella.

A few years ago, well 5 to be exact, we ended up leaving late in the day on our trip to Osoyoos. Once we got to Manning Park we decided to call it a night and finish the rest of the trip in the morning. To our surprise, when we woke up, we found hundreds and hundreds of marmots all over the place. We happened to have some donuts left over from the day before so we fed them to the marmots, which were very tame.

Now each year, we leave later in the day on purpose so that we can spend the night in Manning Park and then wake up to feed the marmots. Tristan and Isabella now enjoy this aspect of our trip, more than anything else.

The essential elements of a scrapbook page are simple: your photos, your journaling, pretty papers.

MORE INSPIRATION   This scrapbooker used just two solid-color papers—a sweet purple and green—in her CHRISTMAS TRADITION #4 design (OPPOSITE), which is the last in a series of four she did about her family's holiday traditions. To finish this done-in-minutes layout, beaded snowflakes were attached with adhesive dots so that they appear to fall gently down the page edge.

GARDEN OF OLD. These vintage farmyard objects (ABOVE LEFT) have been handed down through three generations of this scrapbooker's family, residing now in her backyard. After adhering the three short journaling strips to the page, hand-stitched accents were added using brown embroidery floss and a sewing needle; the floss ends were then glued to the back of the page.

MARMOTS. This photo (ABOVE RIGHT) from the family's yearly vacation was a favorite of the scrapbooker's, so she boldly enlarged it and made it the centerpiece of the page. Don't forget to date your pages; here, the year "2004" is handwritten in a decorative flower-shaped tag. Putting the "marmots" title right on top of the photo ties the page elements together. You don't need to put the photo through the printer, though; these are rub-on letters.

Five steps for making a scrapbook page

(1) Sort through your photos and choose those that document a favorite story or event. There's no magic number—sometimes you'll need only one photo, and sometimes you'll want a dozen.

(2) Go shopping! Take your photos with you so you can pick out papers and embellishments that will complement them.

(3) "Borrow" a page design. Crafts magazines and scrapbooking books are filled with terrific design ideas. When rendered in different colors and with your photos, the pages will have a look that's all your own.

(4) Choose a title for the page and jot a few notes for your journaling.

(5) Play! Move around the elements on the page. Don't adhere anything permanently until the artist within is completely satisfied.

MORE INSPIRATION On POWER TO HEAL, hand-torn paper—such as the yellow-and-purple strip—adds texture and interest to a page about the magic power of a white face cloth. Yes, getting that ragged-edge effect is as easy as ripping the paper. Practice tearing scraps first. To get a contrasting white edge on a torn paper, choose papers that are colored on one side and white on the other. This title is "written" using peel-and-stick letters.

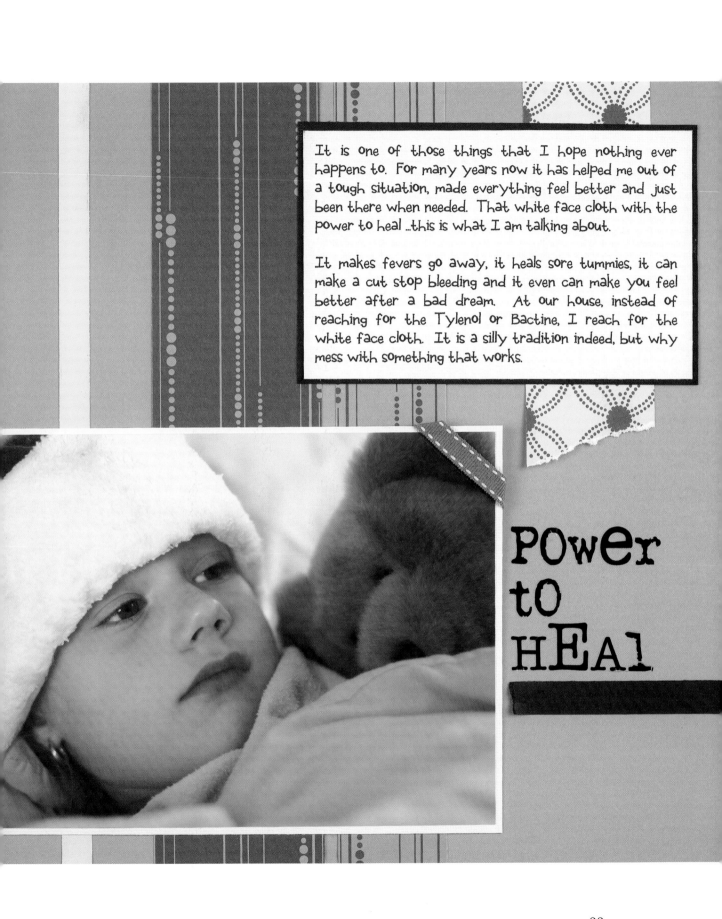

It is one of those things that I hope nothing ever happens to. For many years now it has helped me out of a tough situation, made everything feel better and just been there when needed. That white face cloth with the power to heal ...this is what I am talking about.

It makes fevers go away, it heals sore tummies, it can make a cut stop bleeding and it even can make you feel better after a bad dream. At our house, instead of reaching for the Tylenol or Bactine, I reach for the white face cloth. It is a silly tradition indeed, but why mess with something that works.

POWer
to
hEAl

Leeza's idea starters

To jump-start the pages on your family traditions, ask yourself these questions.

(1) What holidays are your favorites? Grab a calendar and go through it month by month to jog your memory about celebrations such as Christmas, Hanukkah, Easter, Kwanzaa, Thanksgiving, Halloween, Independence Day, and Valentine's Day.

(2) What special things do you do to commemorate these holidays? Is there a special drive you take each winter to see the holiday lights? Do you write a letter to Santa Claus each Christmas Eve? Is your house the favorite stop for neighborhood kids on Halloween? Consider all the details of the days. What kinds of meals do you serve? Is there a dish you're known for, like green-bean casserole?

(3) Don't forget the year's less-celebrated days. Do you do something to mark the first day of spring? The start of baseball season? Do you throw a big party for the Super Bowl?

(4) How do you celebrate major events in your family? Some important dates might be the first and last days of the school year, birthdays, baptisms, and anniversaries.

(5) Are there things your family does year after year, even if you haven't officially called them "traditions"? Sit down with your photos to get your thoughts moving. Do you vacation at a certain cabin on the lake each summer? Do you order pizza and watch a movie with the kids every Friday night?

Essential tools

All of the scrapbook pages in this book were made with simple techniques—cutting, taping, and gluing—and these basic tools.

CUTTING TOOLS. These are key for shaping photos and paper.

SCISSORS. Find a pair with sharp, narrow points for fine cutting.

PAPER CUTTER. Updated, streamlined, and miniaturized, it's invaluable for cutting straight edges and measuring as you cut.

CRAFTS KNIFE. With a sharp, fine blade, it's excellent for cutting out photo mats. It's also handy for positioning small elements, such as stickers, in precise spots.

ADHESIVES. Toss out your old rubber cement! Scrapbooking adhesives will affix your photos and embellishments without causing them to yellow or fade. Like your papers, all adhesives should be acid-, lignin-, and PVC-free.

DOUBLE-SIDED TAPE. It comes in different widths in handy dispensers that make it easy to use. Just feed it through the dispenser, then touch it to the back corners of your photos. Position the photos in place and press lightly to adhere.

REPOSITIONABLE GLUE TAPE. Change your mind (and your layout) without mess.

GLUE STICKS. They make it simple to control the amount of adhesive you apply.

PHOTO SPLITS. Apply these small squares just as you would double-stick tape, then peel off the backing to expose the other sticky side.

PHOTO CORNERS. Use them just as your grandmother did in her photo album.

JOURNALING PENS. Make sure they're pigment or permanent ink, acid-free, lightfast, fadeproof, waterproof, and nonbleeding. Buy a variety of tips. Fine points are ideal for captions and stories; rounded tips are perfect for accents and titles; and calligraphy points make elegant decorative lettering.

RULER. Pick one with a metal edge to measure paper and use with a crafts knife.

PUNCHES. They're like the old paper punch, but updated with high style. Use them to make all sorts of paper shapes, from hearts to hexagons.

Tell me about ...
the things you love

I love my pets, especially my yellow Labrador retriever, Crystal. Crystal represents what I'd like to think are the best parts of myself: She's patient, eternally optimistic, perpetually loyal, unfailingly enthusiastic, and dependable. I chose to do two scrapbook pages about her because I think that loving Crystal reveals a lot about my character.

Quick, name five things you love, other than the people in your life. Don't edit yourself. Be free and fun. What did you come up with? I love doo-wop. We used to call it "beach music," and it was the soundtrack to many summers I spent as a teenager on the South Carolina shore. A song by The Drifters or The Platters can transport me back to a time in life when I was carefree and courageous. I love collecting miniature picture frames. I love a bubble bath. It's a luxurious, silky escape and one of the most decadent indulgences known to womankind. It's my sanity saver, and my family has come to appreciate it too because I always emerge from the water a bit more tolerant and open.

I encourage you to share the things you love by scrapbooking them. You'll automatically elevate their importance and give them greater value in your family structure. Tell the story of your well-worn flannel shirt, your grandfather's book of poems, a classic car, or a flower garden. Do you love your collections? Whether it's stamps or sunglasses or antique clocks, we all seem to collect something.

Scrapbooking about the things you love also helps to define who you are for your family and friends. Take my sister, Cammy. She adores opera music. I don't get opera at all, but she loves

One way or another, we all search for meaning in our lives. I think you can find it by looking at what you do, who you love, and how you spend your time. That's why I love scrapbooking almost as much as I love Crystal, my yellow Lab, and Mikey, my black Lab. Pouring over photos and mementos is probably the best therapy you can find.

STORYTELLER

"Journalist" or "reporter" were words too fancy for my dream; I have known since I was in the 6th grade that I wanted to be a storyteller. Whenever I speak into a microphone or in front of a camera, my curiosity is unleashed and I find my best self. It's what I love most; being a conduit through which other people's stories find their way into the world.

to put a Pavarotti CD on the stereo and get in the kitchen and cook her cares away. Take the time to share your passions with those who love you. I'll bet some of the people closest to you are clueless when it comes to your heart's desires.

If you're still scratching your head and saying to yourself, "I don't have any hobbies, and I'm not sure what I love," then do this: Whenever you are happy, pause for a moment to take inventory of the situation. Look around and make a mental note of who is with you, where you are, and what you are doing. We all have those moments of feeling really connected to life and totally in the groove. That's where you'll find what you love. Sometimes you have to stop what you're doing and be still enough to listen, and you can feel your life's purpose and its passions. I know it sounds far-fetched to some of you (my husband has rolled his eyes at this notion a few times), but scrapbooking will help you gain clarity about your values and beliefs.

STORYTELLER. Subtle layering of papers gives depth to this page. There are as many as five layers total, but sticking to just a few colors keeps the design calm and refined. Because the photos of me were taken on two different days, the colors of my outfits didn't quite work together. The solution? Use one photo in color (and pull the page's color palette from that) and convert the other two to black and white.

Of course my scrapbook of things I love wouldn't be complete without a page about speaking into a microphone or in front of a camera. I love being a conduit through which other people's stories find their way into the world. I've known since I was in the sixth grade that I wanted to be a storyteller. It's how I've made my living. I've been privileged to interview movie stars and rock stars, politicians and preachers. In my private moments, I've spent my life sharing the stories of my family and friends. Communicating a message is what I truly love most. The topic or medium doesn't matter. That's why discovering scrapbooking was like finding a missing piece of my soul. At its essence, it's another way to tell stories.

cuddly

Crystal

The kids named her Crystal and we fell instantly in love with her when my husband brought her in with a big red bow on Christmas morning. This dog has put up with the indignities of being dressed as Buzz Lightyear, Barbie and Batman. She has run to the top of the mountain with us and slept at our feet, always with the same loving disposition and eagerness to please.

CRYSTAL. One of the most important parts of any scrapbook page is the journaling. It gives more life to your pictures. So write down your thoughts. Your voice should resonate, so try not to use phrases or words that aren't "you." Journaling doesn't have to be formal or time-consuming. It can be a caption, a list, a memory, a joke—or just three sentences, which is what I did here.

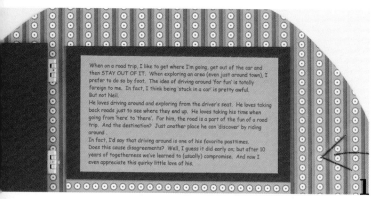  

HIDDEN JOURNALING. It's a fun addition to any page. Borrow these clever ideas. (1) On AROUND HE GOES (OPPOSITE), about a husband's love of exploring big cities and little towns from the driver's seat in a car, the hidden journaling allows the page's simple circle design to shine. Notice how the curved paper echoes the shape of the steering wheel and plays off the title. To make the booklike journaling, cut two identical rectangles out of burgundy card stock. Print out the journaling on cream card stock, mat it with one piece of the burgundy card stock, and adhere it to the scrapbook page. Mat the photo with the second piece of burgundy card stock; attach it to the page using metal hinges (available at scrapbook stores) so it lies directly on top of the journaling. Stitch an arrow onto the background to draw attention to the hidden words. For more stitching techniques, see page 47. (2) On DAD IS MY HERO (PAGE 17), journaling is hidden beneath the photo, which flips up. Mat the main photo with card stock. Then create a paper "hinge" that matches the background paper using a 2"-wide strip of card stock folded in half. Adhere half of the paper hinge to the layout and the other half to the photo. Add a "lift" tag to the photo. (3) On CRISIS CAKE (PAGE 75), part of the journaling is handwritten on a small piece of paper. That paper is folded and tucked into a small sheer fabric envelope, which is adhered to the layout.

MORE INSPIRATION   Though the story behind the photos is always important, sometimes you'll want a page design like this AROUND HE GOES page (OPPOSITE) that hides the journaling—perhaps because the words are private or because it makes the page look less busy or because it's a great way to make the layout interactive.

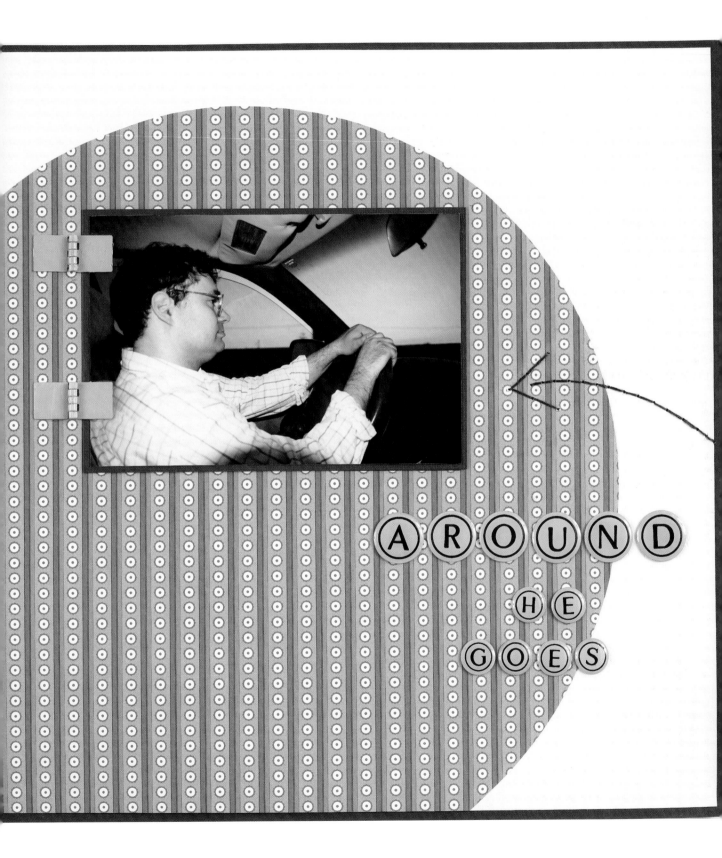

AROUND HE GOES

Even when I don't have a real garden I always try to grow a tomato plant or two. Not only do I see this as a tasty proposition, but it's also one that makes me feel connected to Mom and my childhood. In fact, just the act of growing them makes ME feel as if I'm being a better mother.
Why?
Well, nostalgia, of course!
Just the sight of the bushes reminds me of Mom and the gardens she's kept for as long as I can remember. And the smell of a leaf rubbed between my fingers or a stem brushed?! Why, it can make me feel happy for hours. Then there are the tomatoes themselves. Even my little "I don't like maymoes" girl can't get enough of them sun-warmed and right off of the vine.

Tomatoes

YUM

MORE INSPIRATION These red beauties are the apple of this scrapbooker's eye because they remind her of her mother's garden. "And the smell of a leaf rubbed between my fingers?" she writes on TOMATOES. "Why, it can make me happy for hours." Card stock the color of tomatoes was a logical choice for this layout, along with teal and cream for contrast. Adding the darling "yum" was simple: The little word was printed on vellum, attached to a small square frame (available in the scrapbooking aisles at the crafts store), and adhered to the layout.

The Gordon House—IT'S A VERY SIMPLE HOUSE. VERY SPARE AND MOST NOTEWORTHY FOR ITS GRAPHIC DETAILING. IT'S THE ONLY HOUSE LEFT IN OREGON THAT WAS DESIGNED BY Frank Lloyd Wright AND THAT ALONE MADE NEIL (ESPECIALLY) WANT TO SEE IT. OF COURSE, HE HAS ALWAYS TAKEN THE TIME TO STUDY WHATEVER "BUILDINGS OF NOTE" COME OUR WAY, AND HAS ALWAYS HAD STRONG OPINIONS ON ARCHITECTURE IN GENERAL (THIS IS DEFINITELY HIS MOTHER'S, A VERY TALENTED ARCHITECT HERSELF, INFLUENCE). THIS INTEREST HAS TAKEN US TO MANY IMPRESSIVE PLACES, BUT THERE REALLY WAS SOMETHING UNIQUE, EVEN CREATIVE, ABOUT THIS SMALL BUILDING.

MORE INSPIRATION   A passion for architecture and a trip to a house designed by Frank Lloyd Wright inspired this DESIGN creation. Interesting crops on these vacation photos put the focus squarely on this building's unique design. Don't be afraid to zoom in on just part of a photo (and cut out distractions) if it will make the picture—and the story you're telling—stronger. By weaving together skinny strips of brown card stock, the scrapbooker created a title box that mimics Wright's instantly recognizable style.

Grandma's very colorful blanket now hangs on my wall, but for as long as I can remember (before that) it was kept in my grandparents' rec room/giant basement where our family spent many of the holidays and plenty of 'ordinary' afternoons.

Most of the time (through out food prep and meal time and clean up and board games and conversation) it would hang, ignored, over the back of an old recliner. But at the end of the day, when Grandma would finally sit down to rest, she would drape it across her lap. Today I can still close my eyes and see her sitting there. Quiet and cozy and 'tucked in'. It's an image I treasure and, because of that, the blanket is something I treasure.

Run your page through the sewing machine?

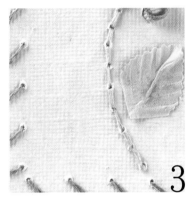
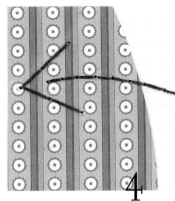

1   2   3   4

SEWING TIPS. Whether done by hand or on a machine, these sewing techniques are an interesting way to add texture and dimension. Practice with scrap papers before putting your layout under the needle. (1) The zigzag stitches on GRANDMA'S BLANKET (OPPOSITE) are easy to hand-stitch. Using an embroidery needle, poke two rows of small holes at regular intervals around the perimeter of the photo. Use a ruler as a guide, if desired. With the needle and two strands of embroidery floss, stitch a simple zigzag along each side. Affix loose ends to the back of the layout. Note: Embroidery floss comes with six strands. Choose how many strands to use based on the desired thickness of the stitches. (2) On TEA FOR TWO (PAGE 105), the precise stitches were created with a sewing machine. Yes, you read that right! Thread the needle and bobbin with a colored thread, select a zigzag stitch, then sew along the seams of the design. Note: Card stock is easiest to sew. Be sure to adhere all paper elements together before sewing. (3) The flower stem on SHE CAN TRY (PAGE 90) was hand-stitched using embroidery floss. (Prepunch holes using an embroidery needle before sewing.) A whipstitch adds the finishing touch to the perimeter of the tag. (4) To draw the reader's attention to hidden journaling on AROUND HE GOES (PAGE 43), a skinny brown arrow was hand-stitched to the page using one strand of embroidery floss.

MORE INSPIRATION   To get the right images for GRANDMA'S BLANKET, the scrapbooker moved in close to this vintage fabric (OPPOSITE). One photo was used whole; a duplicate was cut into small squares.

Absolutely! Little stitches are an artistic addition to any scrapbook.

Leeza's idea starters

To jump-start the pages on things you love, think big and small and ask yourself these questions.

(1) What are you passionate about? Make a list of your hobbies, both ones you actively pursue and those you'd like to spend more time on. What hobby would you like to start?

(2) If you had an unexpected vacation day, what would you most like to do?

(3) What's your most prized possession? What's the one thing (after your family and pets, of course) that you'd save if you knew your house was going to burn down? A wedding ring? A photo? A baseball card?

(4) What's the oddest thing you ever bought?

(5) What is your spouse or partner passionate about?

(6) Do you have a boat? A cabin? A pet?

(7) What's your job? Is it also your passion?

(8) What treasured things have you inherited? Furniture, jewelry, a pet parakeet, an old guitar? Do they remind you of their former owners?

(9) What are your all-time favorite things to do on the weekend? Take out a boat? Read the Sunday paper?

(10) As you go through your photos, what thoughts come to mind? Write just one sentence about each picture.

Layout and design

The beauty of scrapbooking is its individuality; there is no right or wrong way to do it. Each page is as one of-a-kind as you are, tying together your memories and creativity in one unique package. That said, here are a few suggestions (not rules!) to help you create timeless, classic designs.

ELEMENTS OF A PAGE. Start with the basics—photos, papers, and journaling—and build from there. Scrapbooking is as simple (or as complicated) as you want it to be.

KEEP IT SIMPLE. If you're a first-time scrapbooker, begin with solid-color 12"×12" card stock as the base of your page, then add patterned papers and embellishments. Don't affix anything permanently until you're happy with the entire layout. Look for repositionable adhesives that don't penalize you—or wreck your layout—if you change your mind.

CHOOSE COLORS. It almost goes without saying, but if you choose paper colors you love, you'll likely be happy with the results. Pull at least one color from your photos; it'll create instant harmony. Does your dog wear a red collar in the picture? Play up that color. Don't be boxed in by tradition either. Rich reds and greens may be traditional Christmas colors, but that doesn't mean that a holiday page in pastel purples and greens isn't equally beautiful and appropriate. After all, holiday cookies come in all sorts of sweet colors, right?

MIX PHOTO SIZES. Choose one photo to be your focal point; that one should be the largest. Then mix in pictures in other sizes.

DON'T GO OVERBOARD. Stick to just a few colors and patterns. Otherwise you run the risk of overwhelming the photos and the journaling, which should be the real stars of the page.

Tell me about ...
life's difficult lessons

We all want our children to have safe and happy childhoods, free from adult responsibilities and stresses. We want to allow them to spread their wings with a foundation of security. It doesn't always happen. I was ecstatic when I was pregnant with my first child, a girl I named Lexi. Newly wed and wildly optimistic, I hadn't expected the competing traditions and the turf wars that erupted in my marriage to Lexi's father, an English actor whom I had met in New Zealand. My mom tried to tell me that the relationship was moving too fast. But with the impulsiveness that often interferes with the reasoning of young lovers, we plunged in. By the time the baby came, we were sinking fast.

Most people who have been divorced will tell you that no matter how right the decision was, it's still a conflux of guilt and disappointment that never quite leaves you. Of course, I had my darling Lexi, and her happiness was all that mattered to me. Why should she have to feel one moment of pain because of my mistake? How would I explain to her what had happened?

Knowing my tendency for revisionist history, I decided that while the emotions were still heavy on my heart, I would write a letter to Lexi explaining what happened. I probed the most uncomfortable places in my soul. I wrote it all down, and then I sealed the letter tight. That was partly to prevent Lexi from reading it until she's old enough (18 is the right age, I think) and partly to prevent me from rewriting it.

Why put such difficult life lessons in a scrapbook? Because scrapbooking gives us a lens through which we can see

I find journaling about the tough lessons I've learned through the years to be therapeutic. And though journaling generally is used to accompany and amplify a story told by photos, it can be used by itself too. If you're tackling a serious issue like divorce or death, you may not have—or want to include—pictures for your scrapbook. And that's perfectly fine.

ourselves in an honest, pure way. When we share our lives, with all the drama and turmoil, happiness as well as fears, things somehow become more manageable.

The easiest way to tackle a topic that's delicate—or even one that's not—is to sit down and write a letter. It's a form that's familiar to everyone, so it takes the pressure off the task of journaling. Plus, it always feels intimate. Simply start off as you would any letter to a friend ("Dear … ") and keep writing. I've found that stream-of-consciousness writing provides some of the most useful insights.

There are three different "voices" you can use to journal. Most people write in the first person: "I love the way you smile when you're sleeping." You can write in the third person, which is a little less emotional and more like just-the-facts reporting: "It was raining the day Lexi had her ballet recital." I like to write in the second person because it's as if I'm talking directly to the reader: "You were so happy wearing your Halloween costume."

Rid yourself of expectations and just write. It's exactly what I did for Lexi's 13th birthday. I wanted to share with her some of the lessons I've learned through the years. Here's part of the letter I wrote, right from the heart. Try it yourself.

"Welcome to the teen years, darling! What an exciting time of self-discovery. Believe it or not, I can remember being 13. I see so much of myself in you, and yet you are such a unique individual. I know your path in life will be yours alone, but there are some universal truths. I'd like to share some of what I know, what I value, and what I wish for you.

"You are blessed. You're a

FOR LEXI. A scrapbook page such as this one about the split with my daughter Lexi's father isn't something I want strangers to read. Consider buying a special album to hold pages like this one. When including an important and sensitive letter, be sure to seal it to prevent anyone from reading it except for the person to whom it's addressed.

For Lexi

To Be Opened at the age of 18

WHEN IN DOUBT, HUG

I've learned that hugs work because they are small. There is nothing global about a hug, no shock wave of ramifications. When you hug, you simply close your eyes and shut out the big, the bad, and the ugly. They work anywhere, in gilded palaces or the smoldering ruins of war. It's the perfect antidote for just about anything.

TROY

physically beautiful girl with a strong mind and body. You're gifted with great talent to sing, dance, and entertain. Never take those things for granted. Celebrate them whenever and wherever you can. Know that your looks are a gift. They will fade into something even more valuable. 'Beautiful young people are accidents of nature, but beautiful old people are works of art.' One of my heroes, Eleanor Roosevelt, wrote that. If you ever need encouragement or direction, read her words. Chances are, you'll find answers there.

"Be a person of quality. Practice joy every day. And gratitude. Affluence, for the moment, is part of your life. It may or may not always be so. Affluence to a joyous person is more about sharing good fortune than fearing its loss. Look for ways to make someone else's life better. A smile, a good deed, a contribution of any sort. But don't do it for credit or recognition. Only you will know if the gesture has come from your heart.

"Finally, remember that chasing a dream is the antidote for a lifetime of lulls. Many of your teen dreams will give way to adult ones, although some will stay the same. Feed them, nurture them, and don't forget to share them with me. I love to see who you are becoming. I will be here for you always and forever, no matter what. Love, Mom."

WHEN IN DOUBT, HUG. I don't get my journaling perfect on the first try. For this page, I scribbled notes on a pad of paper and on my computer before finalizing exactly what I wanted to say. I love the simplicity of this page because it shows off the joy on Troy's face. There are no fancy cuts or folds, and just two embellishments. It proves that simple is often best.

Five ways to get the most from your papers

(1) Never throw away paper scraps. Those small pieces are perfect for labels, border accents, journaling, and punches.

(2) Store remnants in a clear plastic zippered bag. That way they'll be easy to see—and difficult to forget.

(3) When matting a photo—especially a large one—cut out and reuse the part that will be hidden behind the photo.

(4) Throw a paper-swap party with your scrapbooking girlfriends to get rid of patterns you won't use.

(5) Buy the most popular card stock colors (black, cream, and white) in bulk. Split the papers—and the costs—with friends and you'll save big compared to buying papers per piece.

"NO." Photo corners can be used as a purely decorative element. Here, I placed classic red ribbon corners on opposing ends of my photo for a subtle embellishment. Sometimes when I journal, I write more, sometimes less. It only took one sentence to describe this hard-learned parenting lesson.

Lexi

The more difficult parenting comes when the answer is "no."

Leeza's idea starters

Life is full of peaks and valleys, and we often learn the most from the low points. What tough lessons has life taught you? To jump-start your pages, ask yourself these questions.

(1) Have you ever had to have a difficult conversation with a friend or family member? Perhaps you needed to confront someone about a serious problem.

(2) Have you ever done or said something of which you're ashamed?

(3) Did you have bad habits that you finally kicked? This list can be long, but it doesn't have to include just serious issues. Did you bite your nails? Borrow your college roommate's clothes without asking?

(4) What was your first job? What mistakes did you make because you were new? Think about the deadlines you faced and the times you were forced to make tough decisions. Do you work differently today because of lessons learned long ago?

(5) Think about your children. What parenting mistakes have you made?

(6) We often have friends who come in and out of our lives as we grow and move and have children. What relationship mistakes have you made? Have you been on the receiving end of bad behavior?

(7) What's been your biggest failure so far? What did you learn from it? If you could go back and change the past, would you? Or was that mistake valuable in shaping your character and who you are today?

Letter perfect

Technology has changed the nature of letters, making old ones more precious and new ones easier to capture. Here are some ideas for incorporating them into your scrapbooks.

OLD FAMILY LETTERS. Letters from times past may be brittle, yellow, or faded. To preserve them, photocopy them onto acid-free paper and affix them to your scrapbook pages. Or place the original letters in protective sleeves that you can insert into your scrapbook. Supplement the letters with photographs of the writers or of the people or places mentioned.

ENVELOPES. If you're using old letters, don't forget to tuck the envelopes in protective sleeves too, or make copies of them. The postmarks and stamps are part of the history and should be preserved along with the letters.

POSTCARDS. Like letters, postcards can be inserted in their original form or copied so you can show both sides on a scrapbook page. Consider making extra copies of the signature, the stamp, or the photo in different sizes to use as design elements.

E-MAILS. Our 21st-century computer-generated letters have history all their own. Print out e-mail correspondence that tells a story. For instance, a friend on a round-the-world tour could provide an online travel diary. Print the messages on acid-free paper. And don't forget to include the e-mail subject headings and "From" and "To" lines, as they're part of the history too.

CARDS. Holiday, birthday, or "just because" cards can be incorporated. If you're not sure if a piece is acid-free, enclose it in an archival envelope.

SPECIAL CORRESPONDENCE. Do you want to document your daughter's first year in college or a parent's extended trip to China? Ask them ahead of time to take digital photos and to send you letters about their experiences—then make copies of the letters you write in return before you mail them off. Voilà! All the journaling is written.

Tell me about ...
you, you, you!

My children can't believe that I used to jump out of airplanes, race cars, and hang glide. After all, I'm the mom who freaks out when they forget to put on sunscreen and has a meltdown if they don't wear helmets when skateboarding. Me, tell a naughty joke? They'd never buy that! And that's OK. Now is my time to be a "regular" mom (as they say) versus a showbiz mom.

I'm not saying that my life is stagnant or boring, but it's appropriate that we dance different dances at various stages of our lives. That's why I encourage women to create what I call a "many faces of me" scrapbook page. Find the photos that tell your story, and reconnect with all the dimensions that make up that complex creature called you. Are you a wife? A mother? A risk taker? An avid reader? A gardener? A pack rat? A neat freak? I meet women every day who have forgotten that they have a spirited, spontaneous side. They spend more time thinking about what to make for dinner than they do getting in touch with their own lives. By rewinding through your life and chronicling its highlights, this scrapbook page will help you appreciate your diverse talents and interests. It will help you respect and love what you've done and the choices—good and bad—that you've made. Giving your family the gift of knowing that you had a life before them will help them appreciate the entirety of who you are.

One reason I wrote this book was to reach out to women who want to scrapbook but believe that it's too complicated and time-consuming. To prove it can be easy, fun, and fast—even for first-timers—I invited three of my girlfriends who had never scrapbooked before to make a "many faces of me" page. I gave them pretty papers, great embellishments, and basic tools, all from my Leeza Gibbons Legacies scrapbooking line, then set them loose. The results were as unique as these dynamic women. Take a look at their first attempts—and mine—on the following pages. My friends are hooked!

Let's hear it for the girls! I love sharing tales of past adventures with my girlfriends (FROM LEFT) Holly Tyrer, Jessica Weiner, and Beth Hymson. They know a side of me that's never seen by my kids.

FACES

many

Wife and Mom

Glamour Girl?

Adventurer

Leeza Gibbon

Give your family the gift of knowing you had a life before them. It will help them appreciate the complex creature that is you.

Business Woman

Red Carpet Veteran

me

of

Domestic Diva?

Beauty Expert?

MANY FACES OF ME. Two of the photos on this two-page layout were cut into silhouettes, adding variety to the design. Simply cut carefully around the outside of the person or item you'd like to spotlight. Creative layering of the silhouetted grade-school photo unites the yellow border to the purple paper.

Future Actionists

Women with Attitude

BAND OF ACTIONISTS →

I'M AN ACTIONIST
I'M AN ACTIONIST
I'M AN ACTIONIST
I'M AN ACTIONIST

I'M AN ACTIONIST
I'M AN ACTIONIST

SISTER ACT-IONISTS

Actionist: Someone Who...

INSPIRES

MOTIVATES

WALKS Their TALK

I knew my friend Jessica Weiner would be a natural for this scrapbooking challenge.

After all, she's a writer who is accustomed to telling the story of her life. She's also the walking, talking, laughing, loving personification of empowerment. Her book, *A Very Hungry Girl: How I Filled Up on Life and How You Can Too*, is a candid account of the weight and body issues—and the shattered self-esteem that can go with them—that have shaped her character. (That's Jessica and me, BELOW, at her book signing in Los Angeles.) Jess not only made peace with her own demons, but she made it her battle cry to empower all women to fill up on life and face what's eating them.

Because Jessica is a brilliant communicator, with depth and warmth, I wasn't at all surprised by her scrapbook pages. She is a self-described "actionist." I love that word, don't you? Not quite satisfied to be called a motivator or expert, Jessica coined that word to describe those who take

action to make themselves—and the world—better. As she tours the country speaking to teens and young women, she is creating a sea of actionists. I believe she is changing the world or at least healing it one life at a time. Tell your story, Jess. And along the way, put it all in a scrapbook. That perspective will show you what a true original you are.

ACTIONIST. Metal-rim tags in circles, rectangles, and flower shapes make the journaling task simple for first-time scrapbooker Jessica, who expressed herself in browns and pinks.

Whenever I lose faith in the human spirit, I look to my friend Holly Tyrer, whose journey toward reinvention is as profound as it is painful.

It was 1997. I was hosting and producing my *Leeza* talk show. I had no idea that in the audience one day was a frightened, fragile young woman named Holly. She had seen my show in her native England and had left her troubled home there to start over in the United States. All she had was a map of Hollywood; the name of Paramount Studios, where I taped my show; and some last-ditch hope. Though I didn't know it at the time, I was the hinge upon which her whole plan rested. She would tell you I helped save her life. I will tell you that she helped illuminate mine. Holly was needy and suffering, but she had a spark. By sheer willpower, she was able to step out of that audience and do something most women cannot: She articulated her problem and asked for help. By telling her story of abuse and mental illness, she set her own course toward triumph. And triumph she did, getting a job, getting well, getting strong enough to face her family, and getting

a degree from UCLA. From homeless to happening! At her graduation, I sobbed with the awareness that I had witnessed a miracle.

As you can see on Holly's page, she found her key to happiness in service to others. She is strong, radiant, and powerful. I keep the picture of Holly at her graduation on my office desk. Whenever I think "I can't," I look at her and know I can.

HELPING OTHERS. Holly was lucky to have many photos of herself, but she may be the exception. So many women have told me they aren't in pictures because they are always the ones taking them. If you're absent from photos, make it a point from now on to get *in* the picture more often.

HELPING OTHERS

When I first arrived in America I was all alone, struggling through each day just trying to survive. With my mind and body caving under the pressures of past memories and depression my future didn't look bright; I didn't have a future. Then Leeza came into my life, then Cary and Brandi: Three individuals who were pulling for me to get better, there for me when I couldn't go on alone anymore. With their love and support I got through the hardest time in my life…and now I am able to help others in need. Whether it's helping a friend out or raising money for worthy causes, I am able to pass on the love and support that I received from Leeza, Cary and Brandi to make a difference in other peoples lives.

HELPING OTHERS MAKES THE WORLD GO ROUND

Me & my special 3!
UCLA graduation
2003

Jeff & I
AIDS Marathon,
New Orleans
2004

Leeza & I
Memory Walk
for Alzheimer's
2002

Andy, Coco & I
Revlon Walk for
breast/ovarian cancer
2004

Beth Hymson and I have been friends ever since our freshman year in college. We were sorority sisters in Delta Delta Delta at the University of South Carolina. I remember pledging because I wanted a sisterhood of support, a place to belong that would help make sense of a big campus and a bigger world. Beth was one of the girls who made up my safe world. She was comfortable in all situations, and she seemed wise and experienced to me. When I look at pictures of us from those Tri-Delta days, I can see the hopefulness in our eyes. (That's me, BELOW, on the left; Beth is on the right; and my "little sister" Leslie Bennett is in the middle.) The faces have changed, but much has not. I know I can still count on Beth, no questions asked. What I didn't know then was that Beth and I would share the same personal heartbreak.

Beth's father died of Alzheimer's disease, and it was our parents' shared suffering that brought us back into each other's lives. I asked Beth to use scrapbooking to help sort through some of her feelings. I know how meaningful scrapbooking can be for families in a crisis with a memory dis-

order. "Just put together a page about who you are and where you came from," I told her. She ended up doing many pages of precious moments in her life. "It was so much fun and so easy," she said. Now I can welcome Beth to a new club of sorts—the sisterhood of scrapbookers.

PAWLEYS ISLAND. To hold a vintage black-and-white photo in place, Beth created her own photo corners out of small strips of purple ribbon. Don't mount an original old photograph to a page with adhesive. Either use photo corners so the photo can be removed without damaging it or make a copy of the photo to be used in a layout. Though you may not think of mixing these bold patterns in your clothing, the contrast on a scrapbooking page is dynamic. Experiment by pairing stripes with circles, florals with plaids, paisley with diamonds, and more.

Leeza's idea starters

To come up with things to include on scrapbook pages all about you, ask yourself these questions.

(1) What does your name mean? What's your nickname? What historic events happened the year you were born?

(2) What's your philosophy on life? Are you a "glass half-empty" or a "glass half-full" kind of person?

(3) What was your favorite subject in school?

(4) Are you a cat person or a dog person?

(5) What's your favorite color? Least favorite?

(6) If you were stranded on a desert island, what three things would you bring?

(7) What's your favorite childhood book? Adult book? Movie? Favorite song? Favorite food?

(8) Where would you like to retire?

(9) What's your greatest accomplishment? What is your greatest fear?

(10) What is the natural color of your hair?

(11) If you could change one event in your past, what would it be?

(12) Who is your hero?

(13) If you could trade places for one day with any person, dead or alive, who would it be?

Photo fundamentals

Photographs will be the foundation for almost every scrapbook page you make. Get what you need with these tips.

CARRY YOUR CAMERA EVERYWHERE. That way you're always ready to capture a moment, no matter how small.

TAKE PHOTOS IN A SERIES. Consider times that often aren't recorded, such as a child's waking moments or preparations for an evening meal. Try capturing continuous action too, such as a pickup game of tag football or a dog running to catch a tennis ball.

SNAP PHOTOS WITHOUT FACES. Photos don't have to show people's faces to be interesting. A picture of a child walking away from you or a pair of muddy hands might tell an even better story.

TAKE SCENIC PHOTOS. Picturesque views from trips often can stand on their own. Though the photo of the mountaintop is a logical choice, also think of unusual shots, such as the sign outside the restaurant you loved, the baseball park's marquee, or an empty stretch of highway.

DON'T BE AFRAID TO CROP. Cropping is simply the process of cutting off parts of a photograph. How do you decide what to crop out? Think about whether the background adds to the picture or detracts from it. At first, it may be difficult to cut into a photograph. Make duplicates until you become comfortable with the process. With the right software, cropping can be done on the computer too. Zero in on a particular element of a photograph and enlarge it, or cut it out and combine it with elements from another photo.

REMEMBER TWO IS BETTER THAN ONE. When developing photos, go ahead and order doubles if you don't have a computer scanner at home. That way you'll always have extra photos ready to be scrapbooked.

FORGOT YOUR CAMERA? Buy a postcard to remember the place you're visiting, whether it's a museum, the Grand Canyon, or a famous diner.

Tell me about . . .
lessons from your parents

Oh, sure, there are many ways to deal with a crisis: cool logic, adrenaline-fueled action, spiritual guidance, even instinctual knee-jerk panic. But my mom had a better solution: When there's trouble in the house, bake a chocolate cake.

I don't mean some low-fat, sugarless, flourless lump of bland. I'm talking about a chocolate *cake*, honey. One with cup after cup of sugar, icing so rich it makes your teeth hurt, and real butter. And more butter. My mom's theory on cake baking was simple: When in doubt, throw in another stick of butter. But the point of the cake was not the decadence of the final product. The process of making the cake was what quieted the howling hound known as "the crisis of the moment."

Like any family, we had our share of heartache, trouble, and drama. Some situations were more life-changing than others. But all, in their moment, were of crisis proportion. Each meant it was time to bake a cake. As I measured ingredients, Mom would watch with the eye of a wolf. "Fifty stirs with a wooden spoon" did not mean 51. I would understand later that all that persnickety exactness was my mom's way of giving me something new to focus on. She was orchestrating diversion. Somewhere between the breaking of the first egg and the first bite of chocolate heaven, the yapping crisis went to sleep in a corner.

I know world leaders have all kinds of teams and gear and electronics and diplomatic corps and intelligence agencies to deal with a crisis, and I'm sure it's quite effective. I just wonder if they've tried getting together and baking a chocolate cake.

What did your parents teach you? Think not so much about the lectures you received after breaking a rule but more about

My parents have been married more than 50 years, and I have never heard my father speak an unkind word about my mother, Jean. I grew up watching my mother offer comfort to anyone who needed a strong shoulder. Through their actions, I learned honor and commitment, compassion and kindness. What have your parents taught you? Honor those lessons in your scrapbook.

the quiet ways they parented you that gave you a particular way of viewing the world.

People have a fascination with family trees and genealogy. No doubt there are answers to be found by exploring the past. What's unique about a scrapbook is the opportunity for the past—and all those great lessons our parents taught us—to come alive for future generations. It puts a personal face on the facts that can't live in a news clipping or on a genealogical chart.

Take my dad. He was once a political candidate. It's easy to find old newspaper clippings that chronicle his unsuccessful run for governor of South Carolina. But what the archives don't reveal is his passionate activism and his belief in fairness and freedom. I was just a teenager when he was campaigning. It changed my life traveling across the state "stumping" for Daddy, who taught me the value of integrity and purpose. "You've got to stand for something or you'll fall for anything," he said. I learned from Mom and Dad to set my course, set my resolve, and take action.

Chances are, there is a full history lesson waiting to be unleashed in scrapbook pages about your parents. How comforting it will be to have those images and stories when you no longer have your mom and dad. Please don't worry about not having the exact pictures to match your story. There is no need to be literal. If oak trees remind you of your Dad's strength, use a picture of them. My mom and I loved it when the weather changed. We would watch as the sky clouded over and thunder gathered strength. I wanted to share that love for storms with my family because I think it says a lot about my mom and her fearlessness and the way she embraced change. Obviously I didn't have pictures of her with a storm, so I chose to present our story and our scrapbook pages (PAGE 76) with only the atmosphere.

CRISIS CAKE. I love this color combination of chocolate brown and pink. Shiny brads, which are used on the corners of this journaling box, are one of my favorite embellishments. Just poke a hole with a needle where you'd like to position the brad. Push the brad through the hole and spread the prongs apart on the back of your layout to secure.

CRISIS Cake

Moms always know how to make things better. My Mom always made a chocolate cake. It became known as crisis cake...and it worked miracles for all kinds of emotional maladies and physical ailments. Whenever I have chocolate I think of her and those moments in the kitchen soothing my hurts with sugar!

To Solve Crisis
Bake Cake
1 part encouragement
2 parts support = Mix with
serve!

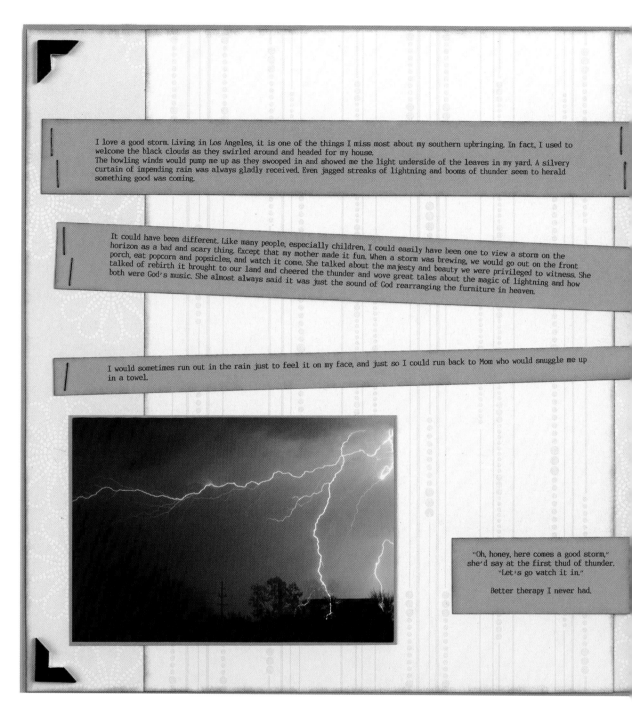

I love a good storm. Living in Los Angeles, it is one of the things I miss most about my southern upbringing. In fact, I used to welcome the black clouds as they swirled around and headed for my house.
The howling winds would pump me up as they swooped in and showed me the light underside of the leaves in my yard. A silvery curtain of impending rain was always gladly received. Even jagged streaks of lightning and booms of thunder seem to herald something good was coming.

It could have been different. Like many people, especially children, I could easily have been one to view a storm on the horizon as a bad and scary thing. Except that my mother made it fun. When a storm was brewing, we would go out on the front porch, eat popcorn and popsicles, and watch it come. She talked about the majesty and beauty we were privileged to witness. She talked of rebirth it brought to our land and cheered the thunder and wove great tales about the magic of lightning and how both were God's music. She almost always said it was just the sound of God rearranging the furniture in heaven.

I would sometimes run out in the rain just to feel it on my face, and just so I could run back to Mom who would snuggle me up in a towel.

"Oh, honey, here comes a good storm," she'd say at the first thud of thunder. "Let's go watch it in."

Better therapy I never had.

Even today, I often reach into my back pocket and pull out some of my mom's homegrown Southern wisdom.

STORM WATCHERS. This journaling was printed on one piece of paper, then cut into strips and set at angles that bring to mind the jaggedness of a lightning bolt. The store-bought letters of the "storm watchers" title were originally round; clipping them with scissors to make them square and irregular gives them interesting movement. To give the papers a dark, smoky look, the edges of each were rubbed with black ink using an ink pad before joining the layout. This design is proof that a scrapbook page can be dynamic and powerful even without photos that exactly document the event.

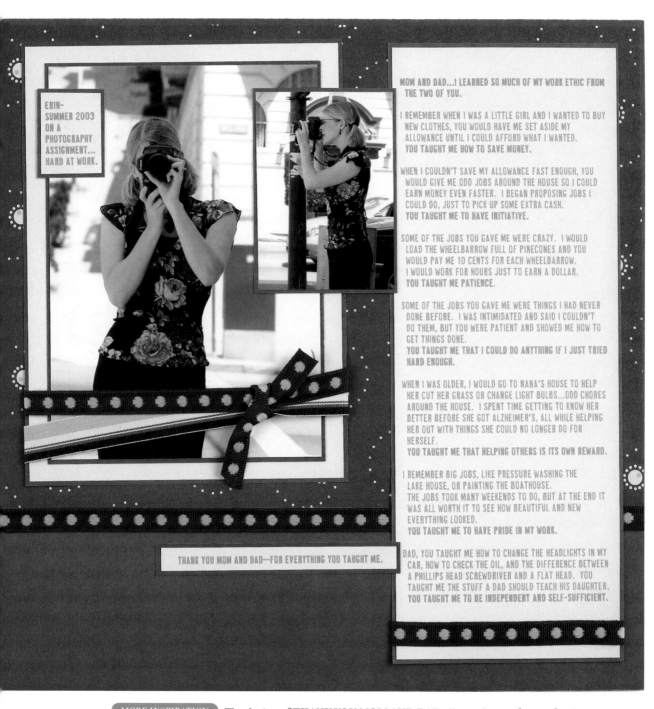

ERIN–
SUMMER 2003
ON A
PHOTOGRAPHY
ASSIGNMENT...
HARD AT WORK.

MOM AND DAD...I LEARNED SO MUCH OF MY WORK ETHIC FROM
THE TWO OF YOU.

I REMEMBER WHEN I WAS A LITTLE GIRL AND I WANTED TO BUY
NEW CLOTHES, YOU WOULD HAVE ME SET ASIDE MY
ALLOWANCE UNTIL I COULD AFFORD WHAT I WANTED.
YOU TAUGHT ME HOW TO SAVE MONEY.

WHEN I COULDN'T SAVE MY ALLOWANCE FAST ENOUGH, YOU
WOULD GIVE ME ODD JOBS AROUND THE HOUSE SO I COULD
EARN MONEY EVEN FASTER. I BEGAN PROPOSING JOBS I
COULD DO, JUST TO PICK UP SOME EXTRA CASH.
YOU TAUGHT ME TO HAVE INITIATIVE.

SOME OF THE JOBS YOU GAVE ME WERE CRAZY. I WOULD
LOAD THE WHEELBARROW FULL OF PINECONES AND YOU
WOULD PAY ME 10 CENTS FOR EACH WHEELBARROW.
I WOULD WORK FOR HOURS JUST TO EARN A DOLLAR.
YOU TAUGHT ME PATIENCE.

SOME OF THE JOBS YOU GAVE ME WERE THINGS I HAD NEVER
DONE BEFORE. I WAS INTIMIDATED AND SAID I COULDN'T
DO THEM, BUT YOU WERE PATIENT AND SHOWED ME HOW TO
GET THINGS DONE.
YOU TAUGHT ME THAT I COULD DO ANYTHING IF I JUST TRIED
HARD ENOUGH.

WHEN I WAS OLDER, I WOULD GO TO NANA'S HOUSE TO HELP
HER CUT HER GRASS OR CHANGE LIGHT BULBS...ODD CHORES
AROUND THE HOUSE. I SPENT TIME GETTING TO KNOW HER
BETTER BEFORE SHE GOT ALZHEIMER'S, ALL WHILE HELPING
HER OUT WITH THINGS SHE COULD NO LONGER DO FOR
HERSELF.
YOU TAUGHT ME THAT HELPING OTHERS IS ITS OWN REWARD.

I REMEMBER BIG JOBS, LIKE PRESSURE WASHING THE
LAKE HOUSE, OR PAINTING THE BOATHOUSE.
THE JOBS TOOK MANY WEEKENDS TO DO, BUT AT THE END IT
WAS ALL WORTH IT TO SEE HOW BEAUTIFUL AND NEW
EVERYTHING LOOKED.
YOU TAUGHT ME TO HAVE PRIDE IN MY WORK.

DAD, YOU TAUGHT ME HOW TO CHANGE THE HEADLIGHTS IN MY
CAR, HOW TO CHECK THE OIL, AND THE DIFFERENCE BETWEEN
A PHILLIPS HEAD SCREWDRIVER AND A FLAT HEAD. YOU
TAUGHT ME THE STUFF A DAD SHOULD TEACH HIS DAUGHTER.
YOU TAUGHT ME TO BE INDEPENDENT AND SELF-SUFFICIENT.

THANK YOU MOM AND DAD--FOR EVERYTHING YOU TAUGHT ME.

MORE INSPIRATION   The design of THANK YOU MOM AND DAD allows plenty of room for the
scrapbooker's journaling about the values she learned from her parents. Ribbons are a beautiful addition
to a page, and you can find them in any color, pattern, or fabric you desire. Look at the scrapbook store
or head to the sewing store for an even more extensive selection. Tie ribbons in a pretty knot, run them
over paper for a border and under the journaling for an accent. Don't cut them too short though:
Glue the ends to the back of the layout if you don't want rough edges to show.

ONE OF THE MOST SIGNIFICANT LESSONS I HAVE LEARNED FROM MY PARENTS IS THE IMPORTANCE OF BEING THERE FOR YOUR CHILDREN-- NO MATTER WHAT.
CRAIG AND I HAVE BEEN THROUGH MANY CHANGES IN OUR LIVES--SOME GREAT AND SOME HORRIBLE--AND THROUGH IT ALL OUR PARENTS HAVE SUPPORTED US UNCONDITIONALLY.
IT'S A WONDERFUL FEELING TO KNOW THAT NO MATTER HOW BADLY WE MESS UP, THEY WILL ALWAYS BE THERE TO HELP US GET BACK ON OUR FEET. THEY HAVE MADE MANY SACRIFICES FOR US OVER THE YEARS AND WE REALIZE THEY WOULD DO ANYTHING FOR US.
NOW THAT I AM A PARENT, I OFTEN FIND MYSELF IN A SITUATION WHERE I DON'T KNOW HOW TO RESPOND. THE EASIEST THING FOR ME TO DO IS TO THINK, "WHAT WOULD MY PARENTS DO IN THIS CIRCUMSTANCE?". THAT IS WHERE I USUALLY FIND MY ANSWER.
IT IS COMFORTING TO KNOW THAT I HAVE SUCH GREAT PARENTS AS ROLE MODELS. WHEN I TALK TO THEM, I FEEL LIKE ALL IS RIGHT IN THE WORLD AND THAT I CAN DO ANYTHING--OVERCOME ANY CHALLENGE.
IT IS A WONDERFUL GIFT THEY HAVE GIVEN ME-- THE GIFT OF CONFIDENCE.
AS I RAISE DAISY, I HOPE I CAN BE HALF THE PARENT TO HER THAT MY PARENTS WERE TO ME. IF SO, I KNOW SHE WILL BE JUST FINE. LUCKY FOR HER, WE GET TO SEE MY PARENTS QUITE OFTEN, SO SHE IS ABLE TO EXPERIENCE FIRST-HAND JUST HOW WONDERFUL THEY ARE.

MIMI AND DAISY SNUGGLING TOGETHER. I TOOK THIS PHOTO AT THE DOCTOR'S OFFICE RIGHT BEFORE DAISY GOT HER 6-YEAR OLD SHOTS. SHE WAS SCARED TO DEATH, AND MIMI WAS THE ONLY PERSON WHO COULD COMFORT HER.

MORE INSPIRATION   Three generations of UNCONDITIONAL LOVE are recognized on this page designed with retro-style papers. After printing the journaling on solid-pink paper, the scrapbooker roughed up the edges with sandpaper to give the layout a subtly distressed look. Go slow to start; you can easily overdo the effect. Mix sanded papers with pristine ones; the contrast will best spotlight the sanded effect.

Leeza's idea starters

To jump-start the scrapbook pages on the lessons you've learned from your parents, ask yourself these questions.

(1) What did your parents teach you when you were a young child? A teenager? In college? After you became a parent?

(2) Were there any things you learned to avoid because of your parents? Such as how to spot and stay away from poison ivy or how to stay out of credit-card debt?

(3) What purely practical things did they teach you? How to drive? How to bake a pie? Paint a ceiling? Iron a shirt? What happened?

(4) What advice have they given you on special days? Think back to your wedding, your graduation, the day you gave birth to their grandchild.

(5) Did your parents teach by example or with words?

(6) What advice from your parents did you not take that you wish you had?

(7) What talents do you have that your parents gave you? Are you a great woodworker? Did your dad like to tinker with computers? Did your mom teach you how to quilt?

(8) What spiritual guidance did they offer?

(9) What advice from your parents have you found yourself passing on to other people? Describe one of those situations. Did the advice work?

Journaling

Second only to your photographs, journaling—which is simply the written words that tell your story—is the key to making your scrapbook a treasured keepsake. Try these ideas to get started.

THE BASICS. When journaling, think of the "who, what, when, where, and why" of the story you're telling.

PHOTO CAPTIONS. Add a caption for each photo or to identify a group of photos. It can be as simple as the location where the photo was taken, the full name of the person pictured, or the date when the event took place.

BULLETED LIST. This is a fun way to add personal details. Make a list of items you took on a camping trip, your dog's favorite toys, or the dishes served at a dinner party you threw.

STORIES. These are treasured memories passed down from generation to generation. They don't have to be long. Use specific details to convey information that the photographs can't. Describe the setting, what people wore, how foods tasted, the sounds in the background, or the way you felt.

POEMS, QUOTES, AND LYRICS. Whether they're your own or were written by someone else, these can enhance a page with a special sentiment. If you use the work of someone else, be sure to attribute it to the proper source. For ideas, head to the library's reference section or do an Internet search based on a particular theme, such as friendship or parenthood.

HANDWRITTEN VERSUS TYPED. Some people avoid journaling at all costs because they feel their handwriting is messy or difficult to read. That's a shame! You can print journal entries from a computer for a neat presentation. Alphabet stencils, stickers, and rub-on letters can be purchased to add to your layouts. But it's important to include your own handwriting on a page, even if it's just a signature or a date written longhand. It's unique to you and will communicate its own message to generations to come.

Tell me about ...
your children's wisdom

There's nothing that can stun you back into reality like the straight talk of a child. Unencumbered by adult inhibitions—and without censors or veils—kids have a way of speaking the truth and delivering it exactly when the adults need to hear it most.

One night around bedtime not that long ago, I was talking through my checklists for the next day, asking the kids if they had their practice uniforms and their lunch money and if they'd finished their homework. My youngest, 6-year-old Nathan, watched me with a bored expression as I organized some bills and scripts.

"Mom, how come you love your job more than me?" Nathan asked. Sting. Stab. There it was: the most painful utterance a working mom can ever hear.

"Honey, what's my favorite job?" I asked him, trying not to sound defensive. "Being my mom," he said. I sent up a prayer of thanks. "But you haven't been working very hard at being my mom lately," he said.

I waited for a moment, realizing that Nathan doesn't care how much effort it takes to organize his life, get him to the dentist and the doctor, make sure his shoes fit and the chores are done, or perform any of the rest of the daily routine that moms all across America do with the precision of a Swiss watch. He was talking about being his mommy, not his mother.

Nathan said he wanted to do more fun things with me. I asked him to draw a picture of what he meant, and he came back with a drawing of a water balloon fight.

We live in a go, go, go world, where life is a series of e-mails, voicemail messages, and instant messages. Sometimes it all zips by without much thought. Scrapbooking puts me in the mind-set to pay attention to life's small moments—such as playing touch football with my boys, Nathan and Troy—as well as the grander ones. Both will become my family's legacy.

Nothing like a kid to speak the truth. Everyday I learn from my children about what matters most. Nathan teaches me hourly the value of play. Uncomplicated, unscheduled time to just have fun. "Come on Mom, take off work and let's have a water balloon fight" I did. Nathan was victorious, but I really won! Lesson learned... Thank You, Nate.

I said what turned out to be the magic words: "How 'bout I take off work. I'll come get you at lunchtime and we can battle it out in the front yard." His megawatt smile triggered a hug with the magnitude of a 7.5 earthquake!

The pictures of our special time found their way into my scrapbook (ABOVE AND OPPOSITE). It was just the two of us. No work, no siblings, no responsibilities. Thank you, Nathan.

I'm astounded sometimes and humbled most of the time by the wise things that come out of my kids' mouths.

I have now come to think of them as centers for continuing education because they often have answers and insights that are elusive to most adults.

One night, after telling my kids for the third time to brush their teeth, pick up their rooms, and put on their pajamas, I saw them looking out the window up at the sky. "Cool," they

NATE'S DAY. I can't live without my digital camera! I loaded these photos into my computer, then sized them to fit my pages. To create the ribbon embellishment (OPPOSITE), cut slits into the paper with a crafts knife, making the cuts slightly wider than the ribbon. Tie two pieces of ribbon into a bow. Center the bow on the page, weave the ends through the slits, and adhere the ends to the back of the page.

listen

In the world of a child the first time he sees a goldfish can be magic, a butterfly is a revelation of immense magnitude but witnessing these brandnew things is only half the thrill for youngsters. the other part is replaying and relaying the passion of a moment. how breathlessly their words pour out. how wide-eyed with wonder their tales are told. how important it all must seem to their little developing brains.

my life is busy. i can't stop everything, delay my schedules. for every whim of my children but i can almost always be more open to listening to what they have to say. not the kind of "uh huh, yes. i see" that comes out with robot-like delivery, but genuinely, enthusiastically listening to what happens in their world.

to do it, you almost always have to be on their level looking them square in the face. you can't be with your back to them at the kitchen sink. you can't have one hand cupped over the phone. you can't have your nose buried in the paper. you've got to be in there in the moment: in their moment.

listen with your eyes.

with your eyes

said. I wanted to drag them away from the distraction, but instead I walked up to the window and asked what they were looking at. "The stars," they said. "Look how bright they are." Then they chanted, "I wish I may, I wish I might, have the wish I wish tonight." Bingo. There it was. One of those magical kid moments that come so free and easy. We took blankets and beanbag chairs out on the terrace and gazed up at the sky together, making up stories. The kids missed their bedtime that night, and their teeth were barely brushed. But I got a much needed reminder of how to live in the moment. And the inspiration for this great scrapbook page (RIGHT).

Tune in to your kids' wisdom. When your child drops some pearl at the pizza place, jot it down so that it's handy when you sit down to scrapbook. I keep a little pad in my purse so I can catch my kids' magic. Put a microcassette recorder in the car and just let it roll. You'll love playing back the arguments and the 10 renditions of "The Wheels on the Bus" you heard on the way to school.

LISTEN WITH YOUR EYES. Look to your photos for clues to what your layout should be. To play up darling Nathan looking intently into a goldfish bowl (OPPOSITE), I used a circle-pattern paper that reminds me of air bubbles. I cut an extra bit of the bubbly paper and mounted it behind a round frame. A clear pebble and fish-shape bead add the perfect whimsical touch.

CATCH THEIR MAGIC
When does it go from magic to mundane? At what age does 'busy' win over 'wonder'? One night this week, after telling my kids for the third time to brush their teeth, pick up their rooms, and put their pajamas on, I saw them looking out the window up at the sky. "Cool," they said. What I wanted to do was drag them away from the distraction, but instead I walked up to the window and said, "What are you looking at?" "The stars," they said. "Look how bright they are." Then they chanted, "I wish I may, I wish I might, have the wish I wish tonight." Bingo. There it was. One of those magical kid moments that come so free and easy. We took blankets and beanbag chairs out on the terrace and gazed up at the sky together, making up stories. The kids missed their bedtime that night, and their teeth were barely brushed a nanosecond. But I got a much needed reminder of how to live in the moment.

What important life lesson did I learn from the example of my 7-year-old daughter's courageous and loving act of kindness for an unknown person in need? That the bigger and harder the sacrifice, the greater the joy and contentment in the giving of it! I think this day will be one of our most treasured memories and I pray that Ashley's spirit of compassion will continue to shine in the years to come...

April 3, 2003

♥ Locks of Love

presents this
Certificate of Appre

to

Ashley Bergman

From the Board of Directors, st
the children who w
from your loving hair dep

I think you are pretty and I think when you get your hair cut you will be pretty still

LOCKS OF LOVE

A few weeks ago, Ashley heard in school about how you can donate your hair to a charity that makes wigs for children with illnesses like cancer. When she came home that day, full of compassion and determined to donate her own hair, I was surprised and—to be honest—a bit skeptical as to whether she was really serious since she adores her long, beautiful hair and is always styling it. When I told her it meant she would have to cut at least 10" off—a drastic change for someone who's never had more than a trim!—she gulped, visibly worked to overcome her shock, and shyly said, "That's okay, Mommy...I won't even care if the other kids make fun of me!" (she's always thought she'd look ugly with short hair). I thought I was going to lose it right then and there! My heart swelled as I watched her bravely go through with it today despite her fears, without a hint of wavering in her decision. Kaitlyn sweetly offered to get her hair cut just as short in support of her little sister and I think they both looked so beautiful with their new hair styles—especially combined with their glowing smiles! Ashley couldn't wait to get home and send her hair off to a little sick girl who would hopefully feel beautiful in her new "Ashley wig" and we're all so proud of her selfless gift of love!

MORE INSPIRATION This pretty-in-all-pink LOCKS OF LOVE layout shows that a monochromatic approach is classic and anything but boring. An envelope adhered to the layout provides a space to store important certificates and notes. You can certainly buy envelopes, but if you want an envelope to exactly match the layout—as this scrapbooker did—then make your own from card stock. Look for envelope templates at the crafts store. Don't seal this envelope; you'll want whoever reads this page to reach in and see what's inside. A pink paper tag embellished with a heart-shape brad makes a handy clasp.

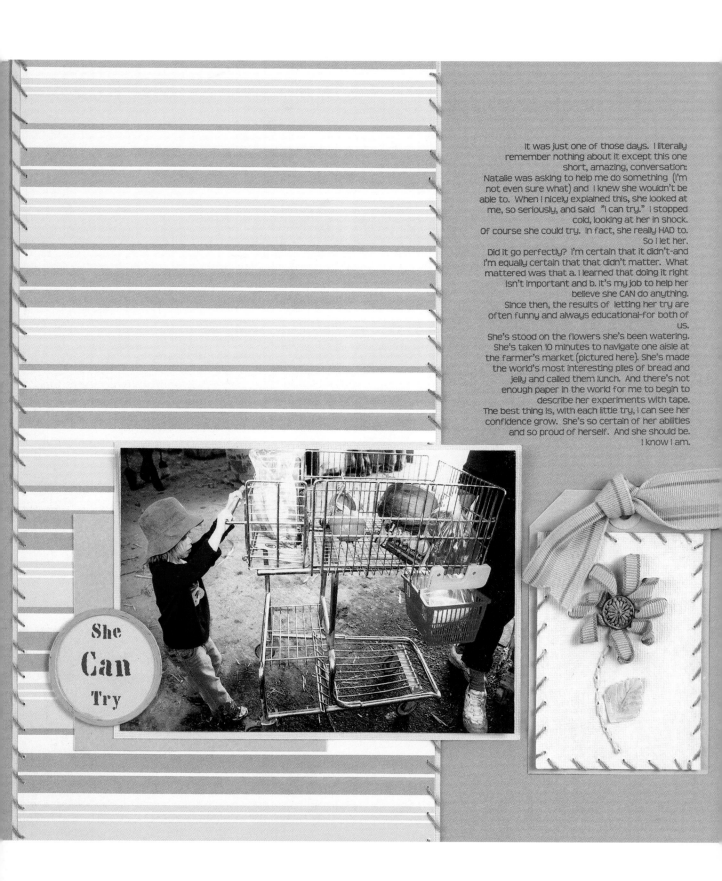

It was just one of those days. I literally remember nothing about it except this one short, amazing, conversation: Natalie was asking to help me do something (I'm not even sure what) and I knew she wouldn't be able to. When I nicely explained this, she looked at me, so seriously, and said "I can try." I stopped cold, looking at her in shock. Of course she could try. In fact, she really HAD to. So I let her.

Did it go perfectly? I'm certain that it didn't-and I'm equally certain that that didn't matter. What mattered was that a. I learned that doing it right isn't important and b. It's my job to help her believe she CAN do anything.

Since then, the results of letting her try are often funny and always educational-for both of us.

She's stood on the flowers she's been watering. She's taken 10 minutes to navigate one aisle at the farmer's market (pictured here). She's made the world's most interesting piles of bread and jelly and called them lunch. And there's not enough paper in the world for me to begin to describe her experiments with tape.

The best thing is, with each little try, I can see her confidence grow. She's so certain of her abilities and so proud of herself. And she should be. I know I am.

She Can Try

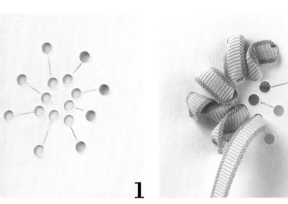

1

2

3

4

FLOWER TAG. If you're feeling adventurous, fashion a pretty flower tag to add texture and dimension to your page. Here's how: (1) To make the flower, you'll need a handheld hole punch that lets you make holes anywhere on a paper. (It's different from a regular hole punch, which only reaches a small distance from the edge of the paper.) Punch eight holes in a wide circle on white paper; these will create the outer edges of the flower petals. Next, punch an inner circle of eight holes, which will form the center edges of the petals. The holes should not be placed symmetrically; unevenness will give a more natural shape to the flower. Use a pencil to draw lines from inner to outer holes. This will help you determine the easiest path for your ribbon and assure that all the holes are used. (2) Starting on the back of the paper, thread the ribbon from inner to outer holes, moving around the flower without skipping any holes. Twist the ribbon now and then and keep it slack, especially in front. (3) Glue the ends of the ribbon to the back of the paper. Add a decorative center, such as a pretty button. (4) Hand-stitch a stem for the flower using embroidery floss, then attach a paper leaf. (For stitching tips, see page 47.) Whipstitch around the edge of the paper with green embroidery floss; mount it on a paper tag; and attach the tag to the layout with a ribbon.

MORE INSPIRATION   When a little one insists "I can try," she inspires her mom to make this SHE CAN TRY scrapbook page (OPPOSITE) about the importance of persistence and believing in yourself.

ADViCE

BE NICE TO DADDY

The thing is, I'm not mean to Daddy/Neil (not often at any rate). Especially not in front of Natalie. But sometimes I do get tired; or distracted; or rushed and I don't sound (or seem) as nice as I should. Maybe I speak too impatiently. Maybe my posture is 'off'. Maybe I seem just a bit grumpy overall and react and respond without tact. I don't know.
But I do know that this is something, a bad habit perhaps, that I have to watch.
How do I know this?
Because of my she-doesn't-know-it-but-she's-super-wise Natalie.
Occasionally, when I'm just talking to Neil, she'll come up and look at me, with confusion or feistiness, and declare that I must "Be nice to Daddy". I'm usually surprised. I was just talking. Which is what I explain to her. And it's the truth.
But deeper than that is another truth-that I need to pay attention to how I treat him (and everyone else). I needed to hear that I can come across as too grouchy when I intend to come across casually. That I can seem critical when I don't mean to...
Maybe this is an even bigger lesson in learning to watch how critical I actually am. But would rather not be.
All this insight just because my little girl pipes in, on occasion, to 'protect' her beloved daddy!
I'm not surprised a bit either. Not only does she often say things that lead me questioning or wondering over something but I know that she and I both know that Neil, that crazy Daddy of hers, is worth protecting (even from accidental neglect).

MORE INSPIRATION Remember those handheld label makers from your childhood? They're terrific for adding little labels to a scrapbook page like GOOD ADVICE. A long, thin strip of orange paper was fed through a label maker to create the subtitle "be nice to daddy." It's adhered to a pink-and-orange ribbon. Using the label maker and another short strip of orange paper, the date "7/o3" was added to a little tag and attached to the left page. Notice how the placement of the vellum title "Good Advice"—which stretches across both pages—makes the two scrapbook pages work as one. Use adhesives designed especially for vellum; regular adhesives may show through the paper.

Leeza's idea starters

Out of the mouths of babes, right? To jump-start the pages on the lessons you've learned from your children, ask yourself these questions.

(1) What did you learn from your newborn? Patience? That you'll never have a neat and tidy house again? That crying can actually be a sweet sound? Think about your children at their different ages.

(2) As your baby grew into a toddler, what did he or she teach you while learning to walk and talk?

(3) What happened when your baby started to talk? When your baby started school?

(4) What actions of your child delighted you? Have you ever been surprised to find out that he or she actually listened to you and learned?

(5) What qualities do your kids' possess that you envy? How do they show their joy? Do they speak their minds? Are they free to enjoy the beauty of a summer rain shower? Do they make friends easily?

(6) If you have teenagers and young adults, what choices have they made that made you proud? Think about their actions in school, on the playing field, at church, and at work.

(7) These topics are certainly not limited to parents with children. Are you an aunt? A teacher? A store clerk? A favorite neighbor? What have you learned from the children you know?

Be a copycat

There are many reasons for making copies of photos and other scrapbook elements. You may want to include the same family picture in scrapbooks for each of your children, for instance. Perhaps you have an article about a family wedding 100 years ago that is falling apart and needs to be preserved. Or you may want to adjust the size of a photo to fit on a page. With home office equipment and your local copy store, you can make as many copies as you need, quickly and for little cost. There's really only one rule: Never cut up an original photo for which you don't have a negative or digital copy.

COPY CENTER. Go to your local store to make low-cost color copies onto acid-free and lignin-free paper. By planning ahead, you can embellish the photos in preparation for scrapbooking. For example, if you have a photo of your family camping in a birch forest, lay a piece of birch bark behind the photo so its pattern will copy as the background.

HOME SCANNER. Many computer printers now come with scanners, so you can scan virtually anything into your computer and print it out. Consider all the possibilities, such as photos, magazine or newspaper articles, brochures, greeting cards, book covers, and more. Once you've scanned the material, you can manipulate it using a software program.

COMMERCIAL DEVELOPER. Take pictures on a CD-ROM to a discount or photo store, which often has stand-alone kiosks where you can print your photos. You can crop the images and print out different sizes instantly.

BLACK-AND-WHITE OR COLOR? When copying photos, take advantage of the opportunity to convert a color photo into black and white. But don't automatically rule out color copies for a vintage black-and-white photo. A color copy may best capture a yellowed or aged feel.

Tell me about...
your everyday rituals

Hugs and kisses abound in my family, even though they are often met with mock protest from the kids. As I help my son Troy with his backpack, I ask, "How much do I love you?" Without hesitation, he replies, "Always and forever," followed by both of us in harmony, "No matter what."

Notes in lunchboxes, phone messages, and letters from home are always signed with those same words: "I love you always and forever, no matter what." Eventually we shortened it to AFNMW. No matter how angry or upset we may be with each other, we can somehow find the breath to utter it, even though it may be with an indignant sigh.

Over the years, this has become a comforting everyday ritual. It's a little thing that makes us feel safe and sound. We all know routine makes children feel better. And this AFNMW routine is almost as good as a SpongeBob SquarePants bandage on imaginary boo-boos, another of our daily rituals.

Troy was away at camp a few summers ago. Even though he was only gone for three weeks, I lived for a letter or postcard from him. When he wrote to tell me about his big adventure of photographing a bear right outside of his cabin (PAGE 100), he signed it AFNMW. It was a hug from far away.

Look for those everyday, ordinary things that you do within your family, and document them in your scrapbook. My mother

You know how they say that love isn't love until you give it away? I think it's the same with pictures. Why do we have all these frozen images if we aren't going to share them and let the emotions wash over us time and time again? That's why a photo similar to this one of Lexi and me was certain to make its way into my scrapbook.

Within the scrapbook layout image:

My mom used to always give me little kisses
before she sent me on my way.
A kiss for luck,
a kiss to remind me how much she loved me,
a kiss to make the hurt go away.

Over the years I got accustomed to these little moments
which were so symbolic of both leaving her
and taking a part of her with me.
I always knew that even when she wasn't with me,
she would hold me in her heart
and keep me safe there.
I rarely felt alone
and found it comforting to know that our love
can transcend locations.

Whenever I give my kids a kiss, I think of mom.

ME WITH MOM

KISSEY FACE

LOVE

I love these pictures!
They represent tradition in the most wonderful sense.

always kissed our foreheads to see if we had a fever. Daddy found that the remedy to most troubles was a washcloth across our heads, either soaked in ice water or dabbed with chest rub. Grilled cheese sandwiches were always on the menu for a sick kid who stayed home from school. I find myself doing the same things for my family. It always makes me smile when I recognize that, dagnabit (that's Southern for "goshdarnit"), I am my mother!

You'll always celebrate the big events in your family's life, and that's great. But it's the everyday moments that will comfort and amaze you. As years pass, a simple lullaby sung each night often becomes a more vivid memory than the most elaborate holiday celebration. These small memories are real gifts we have to pass on.

KISSEY FACE. These pictures (ABOVE) represent tradition in the most wonderful sense. My mom used to give me little kisses before she sent me on my way. A kiss for luck, a kiss to remind me how much she loved me, a kiss to make the hurt go away. Over the years, I got accustomed to these little moments, which were symbolic of both leaving her and taking a part of her with me. I always knew that even when I wasn't with her, she would "hold me in her heart." I rarely felt alone and found it comforting to know that our love could transcend location. Whenever I give my kids a kiss, I think of Mom. Designwise, this page begged for some sweet accents: skinny ribbons, square white eyelets, silver frames, and vellum.

SWEET SLEEP. I had to do a page (BELOW) about my ritual of tiptoeing into each of my kids' bedrooms at night to kiss them—just as my mom had done. The journaling is printed on three pieces of paper that are tucked into vellum envelopes. The photo is so sweet, it's used twice: once in color, once in black and white.

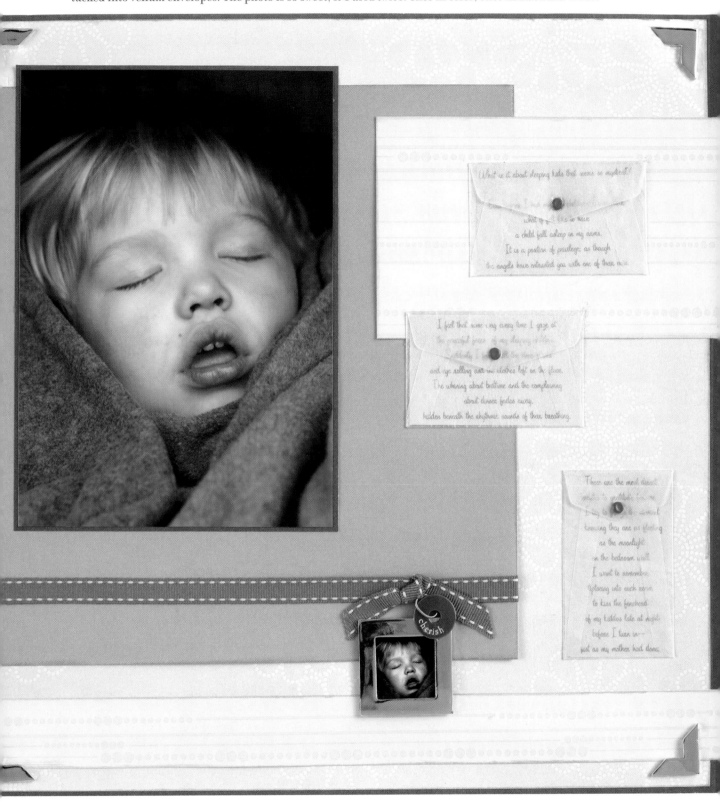

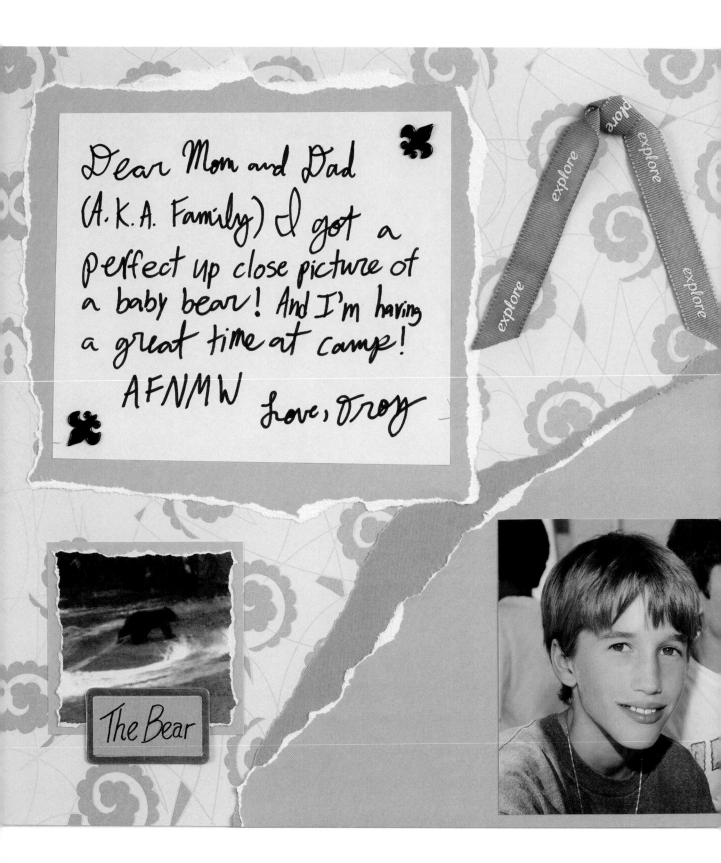

Dear Mom and Dad (A.K.A. Family) I got a perfect up close picture of a baby bear! And I'm having a great time at camp! AFNMW Love, Troy

The Bear

Five ways to banish writer's block forever

(1) Pick up a photo and start asking yourself "who, what, when, where, and why" questions.

(2) Don't worry about grammar.

(3) Write like you talk.

(4) Recognize that no one gets journaling right on the first try. Do a first draft (and a second and third, if needed) on the computer or in a notebook.

(5) Set a timer for five minutes. Write down whatever comes into your head. The only rule is that you cannot stop writing until the time is up.

AFNMW. Tear it up! Ripped paper edges command attention and add depth without actually adding another layer of paper. Pencil in a rough tear line to guide you. Though you can tear any paper, if you'd like to reveal a white edge, choose a paper with color or pattern on one side and white on the other.

Seven never lets me forget that we need to play ball every day.

MORE INSPIRATION A devoted dog, Seven, gets his due on this PLAY BALL page. To print out journaling at a precise place on patterned paper (notice how this type sits right on top of a line of color), first print the words on unlined white paper. (This works best with only one line of type.) Next, cut out a wide strip from patterned paper; attach it with temporary adhesive directly on top of the printed type, lining up the pattern and type as desired. Reload that paper into the computer printer, and print the words again. Unstick the patterned paper—with its journaling—from the white paper and move it to the scrapbook page.

A DAILY *hug*

TRISTAN AND ISABELLA ARE GROWING UP SO FAST AND SEEM MORE SELF—SUFFICIENT EACH AND EVERY DAY. IT WAS NOT THAT MANY YEARS AGO THAT I WAS WISHING THAT THEY WOULD GROW UP AND NOW I AM WISHING THAT THEY WOULD STOP. LUCKILY, THEY ARE STILL NOT TOO OLD FOR A DAILY HUG (OR TEN), AND I FIND MYSELF HUGGING THEM HARDER AND LONGER THAN I DID BEFORE...UNSURE IF SOON THEY WILL NO LONGER WANT TO BE HUGGING MOM ON A REGULAR BASIS.

♡ momma

MORE INSPIRATION   A handwritten date or name—as on this A DAILY HUG page—adds a wonderfully personal touch. In 50 years, the children of this "momma" will still instantly recognize her handwriting.

MORE INSPIRATION The inclusion of a father's favorite daily puzzle adds a unique touch to this CROSSWORD design (ABOVE LEFT). Don't put the newspaper-printed puzzle directly on a page. For archival quality, copy it onto acid-free paper first. (Consider making a color copy if you want to preserve the off-white color of the original.)

LUNCH WITH HIS MOM. This son has lunch with his mom six times a week! Now that's a great family ritual. This layout (ABOVE RIGHT) makes good use of small leftover scraps of paper. Cut strips of varying width to make a wide border down one side of the page. Use a Japanese screw punch to make holes; tie tiny ribbons through for accents.

TEA FOR TWO. Circles are the repeating design on this page (OPPOSITE), pulled from the bottom of the teapot in the photo. Small cups and bowls were used as patterns for paper circles, and a sewing machine stitched the elements together. (For sewing info, see page 47.) Journaling was printed in a circle.

Add whimsy and interest to titles by
mixing uppercase and lowercase
letters in the same word.

2001

Bella —
For our
many tea
parties...
♡momma

For Isabella's birthday in 2001, I made her a tea pot at the local pottery store. Almost every day since that time we have had a pot of tea together. Either in the morning before school with breakfast, after school with our snack or in the evening with cookies, we always find an excuse for a tea party. It is our special daily ritual where we chat, share a pot of English Breakfast tea, and show a little love.

TEA for TWO

Leeza's idea starters

To jump-start the pages about your everyday rituals, think big and small and ask yourself these questions.

(1) What's your daily routine? Mentally walk through your day from morning to night. What do you eat for breakfast? Do you have to have your coffee a particular way? Is there a certain news program you watch to start your day?

(2) What's the first section of the newspaper you read? The comics? The obituaries?

(3) Do you always call your loved one "sweetie" instead of his or her full name?

(4) Do you always put sugar in your cereal?

(5) Is there one person you talk to on the phone regularly? Your mother? A sister? A best friend?

(6) Do you drive the same way to work each day?

(7) Do you take a candy break every afternoon? What's your must-have candy bar?

(8) When your kids return from school, what's your routine? Do you serve a snack? Talk on the back porch about the day?

(9) Do your kids always sit in the same seats in the car?

(10) What prayers do you say at night?

Black-and-white photos

Most photographs today are taken in color, but it's likely that you have black-and-white photos in boxes under your bed or in the closet, including historical photos of family ancestors as well as your own childhood photos. Old or new, photos in black and white bring an elegance and sense of history to your scrapbooking. Here are some ideas for using them effectively.

RESTORING OLD PHOTOS. Historical photos in your collection may be faded, cracked, or torn. To restore them to better condition, you can seek outside help or do it yourself. Commercial services are available that will make a copy of an old photo, retouch it, and make a new negative and print for you. Some restoration can be done at home if you have a computer photo scanner and photo-retouching software. Simply scan the old photo at a high resolution, adjust the midtones and shadows of the image, and use the software program to improve parts of the photo that are seriously damaged or faded.

CONVERTING COLOR PHOTOS. Photographs of special occasions can be converted from color to black and white with little effort. Simply ask your local film developer to make a black-and-white print from a color negative, scan the photo as black and white into your computer, or make a black-and-white copy of a photo at your local copy center. If you take photos with a digital camera, it's a snap to convert the photos to black and white on your computer.

PRESERVING HISTORY. No matter what you do, don't cut or alter an original old photo. Make a color copy first (a color copy will capture the mellowed warmth of a vintage photo better than a black-and-white copy), and keep the original photo in a plastic sleeve or acid-free envelope.

MOUNTING OLD PHOTOS. Never mount a vintage photograph to a scrapbook page with adhesive; even archival adhesives can damage old photos. Instead, use photo corners, so the photo can be removed without damage.

Tell me about . . .
the places you've been

When you travel, don't you sometimes feel that you "belong" certain places? That was true for our family when we went to Bath, England. Actress Jane Seymour and her husband, James Keach, invited us to ring in the year 2000 at their beloved castle, St. Catherine's Court, which presides majestically over the English hillside. We learned archery, went horseback riding, and became very British for a few days. My favorite part was dressing up for a "Lords and Ladies" costume ball on New Year's Eve. My husband, Steve, looked surprisingly at home in a ruffled shirt. My daughter, Lexi, was my lady-in-waiting. And I felt like Guinevere. We snuck out of the party just after midnight, and for our first official act of 2000, we went to the chapel on the grounds and lit candles of hope. Being in a church that also saw the first millennium was spiritual and memorable. I know that trip changed us in a profound way. We were able to get out of our routine to discover that not only do we *love* each other, but we actually *like* being together as well.

When we visit new places, it opens up our minds and our hearts and allows us to get perspective on our lives and our place on the planet. Write about your journeys in your scrapbook. Let your true self shine through. Part of that process is with your journaling, part with your pictures. I've taken almost all of the pictures you see on my pages. Like most moms, there's no professional photographer following my family around.

Travel offers a rich canvas for your scrapbook. Everything's game, from an overseas holiday—that's my husband's grandmother on the camel in front of the pyramids at age 90!—to a weekend getaway at the beach. Here's a favorite trick of mine: Send yourself postcards while you're on vacation. When you start to scrapbook the trip, your journaling will be done.

We ushered in the year 2000 with our friend Jane Seymour and her family at their castle in England. Complete with costume ball and archery (Jane is amazing!) it was a fitting setting for the new millennium. At midnight, Steve and I slipped away to light a candle of hope in the little church on the grounds. It was a once in a lifetime memory.

My point is that the photos taken with a point-and-shoot camera are perfect for scrapbooks.

When Lexi was born, I promised her I would make sure her world was wide open. One of my favorite pictures is of Lexi in her baby stroller outside the Vatican. I knew back then that I would take her back to Italy when she was older and could appreciate it. Thanks to the Leading Women Entrepreneurs of the World, I made good on my word. This nonprofit group, to which I belong, celebrates the resourcefulness, resolve, and resiliency of female entrepreneurs. I want my daughter to be inspired and motivated by other women, so when the annual meeting was announced for Venice a few years ago, Lexi and I signed up. She listened as self-made women from around the world told their stories. So what if she was the only person under 40? They embraced Lexi with open arms and ulti-mately became mentors. Better examples of women's

LORDS AND LADIES. The stay in a centuries-old English castle seemed to call for pages that were a bit more elaborate than my usual designs. A paper punch added Renaissance flair to the corners of my journaling. I made my own embellishments by cutting out paper shapes and making them into stickers.

empowerment I could never find. We both fell in love with Venice.

I loved the opera houses; Lexi loved the shopping. I loved the architecture; Lexi loved the pigeons on the piazza. We both loved the gondolas, but Lexi's favorite part was the water taxi rides. One of the drivers let her get behind the wheel as we sped through the canals. It was something right out of a movie! Now that Lexi's older, I love to travel with her even more. I want her to experience and explore different places, new cultures and ideas. I believe that when we have an appreciation for those outside of our comfort zone, we don't find our global situation so threatening.

VENICE. A color palette of watery blues and greens is a perfect choice for this page (OPPOSITE) about Lexi's and my excursion through Italian canals. It only takes a few design tricks to make the journaling tag that cleverly slides behind (and shows through) a transparent picture. (1) Print a picture—this one is of a Venetian canal—on a transparency sheet. (If you don't have a scanner and printer, it's easy to do this at a copy shop.) Fold back the side edges of the photo about ¼" toward the back; use those edges to adhere the picture to the layout. This will create a photo pocket that the journaling will slide behind. (2) Print the journaling on the back (white) side of a sheet of patterned paper; cut it slightly smaller than the transparency pocket, adding a 2" margin at the top. Fold the paper 1" from the top so the patterned paper shows above the journaling. The folded edge will catch on the pocket's top edge to hold the journaling in place. (3) Cut a long ribbon; secure it to the back of journaling. Cover the back of the journaling and ribbon with contrasting card stock. Secure layers together with a brad. Slide journaling into pocket.

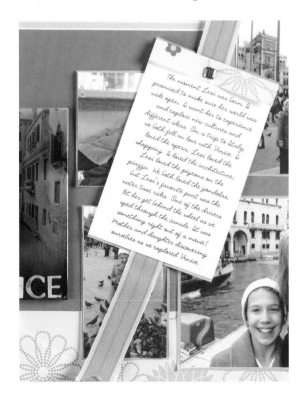

The moment Lexi was born, I promised to make sure her world was wide open. I want her to experience and explore new cultures and different ideas. On a trip to Italy, we both fell in love with Venice. I loved the opera, she loved the shopping, and the architecture... We saw the pigeons on the piazza, rode the gondolas, but Lexi's favorite part was the water taxis. One of the drivers let her behind the wheel as we flew through the canals. It was something right out of a movie! Mother and daughter discovering Venice.

VENICE

A DA
PARA

*Polynesian
Cultural Center*

October '99
Island of Oahu

MORE INSPIRATION Alphabet stamps colored with two shades of blue ink give the title of A DAY IN PARADISE a watery effect that suits the Hawaiian-themed layout. Stamps can be a handy addition to a scrapbooker's tool chest. Use them for titles, on tags, and even for journaling. To match the metal-rim tags to the colors in the layout, the scrapbooker cut the existing paper out of store-bought tags, cut the appropriate shapes from the correct color papers, and adhered them to the tags.

Five ways to find time for scrapbooking

(1) Keep everything in a central location so you can sit down and work on your pages even if you have just a few minutes.

(2) Schedule scrapbooking time into your weekly calendar, just as you would a hair appointment or professional meeting.

(3) Scrapbook while you're watching TV.

(4) Instead of meeting a friend at a restaurant for lunch, plan a scrapbooking lunch at home with take-out food.

(5) Set up a scrapbooking center for your kids with their own supplies so they can work along with you and create their own masterpieces. The pages are great to take to show-and-tell days at school.

MORE INSPIRATION   A store-bought journaling card with elegant stitching along the edge slips into a matching sheer fabric envelope on JAPANESE GARDENS. Beaded accents stashed in the envelope add interest. The lovely ripped-paper effect follows the curved line of the stone staircase in the middle photo. Experiment with different adhesives to find your favorites, and be judicious when using liquid glues. If you overuse some kinds, they may be absorbed into your papers, causing them to warp.

Japanese gardens

The Japanese gardens are definitely 1 of Portland's most unique & beautiful places. Everything from the sculpture to the architecture to the landscape is just amazing and relaxing. I can't praise it all enough.

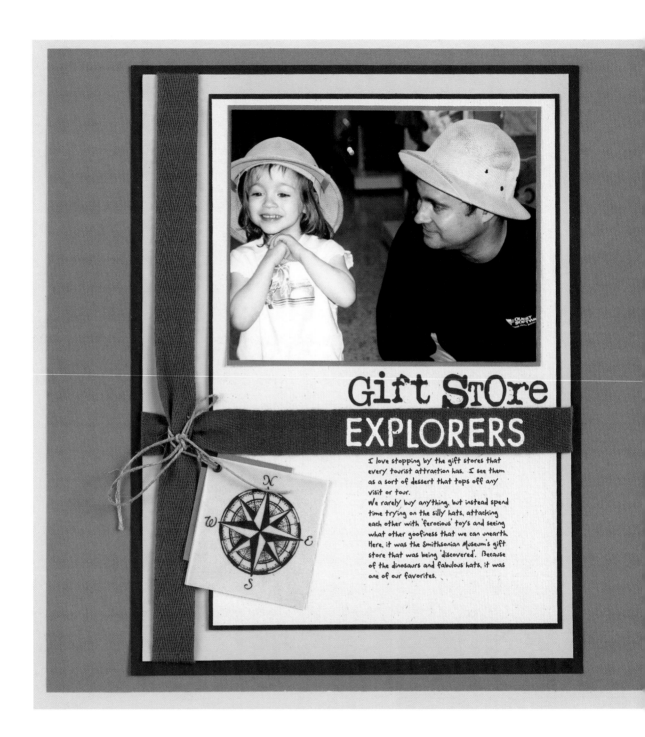

Gift Store
EXPLORERS

I love stopping by the gift stores that every tourist attraction has. I see them as a sort of dessert that tops off any visit or tour.

We rarely buy anything, but instead spend time trying on the silly hats, attacking each other with 'ferocious' toys and seeing what other goofiness that we can unearth. Here, it was the Smithsonian Museum's gift store that was being 'discovered'. Because of the dinosaurs and fabulous hats, it was one of our favorites.

Play the alphabet game! There are many ways to add
Why add a title? It's an important

1

2

3

4

TITLES. (1) The title on the GIFT STORE EXPLORERS page (OPPOSITE) was made with rub-on letters, which you can purchase at a scrapbooking store. They're easy to use: Position a letter on a surface, then rub with a stylus. The liner paper can then be peeled away. For added dimension, the word "explorers" was rubbed directly onto twill ribbon. (2) The vellum letters on GRANDMA'S BLANKET (PAGE 46) are also store-bought. They're affixed to the layout with adhesive. (3) To create the DESIGN title (PAGE 45), sketch letters on card stock, then cut them out using a crafts knife. Need help? Use computer-generated letters as guides. (4) The JAPANESE GARDEN letters (PAGE 117) are easy-to-use stickers.

MORE INSPIRATION The gift stores that populate every tourist attraction are this scrapbooker's favorite place to visit when traveling, as she proves on this GIFT STORE EXPLORERS page (OPPOSITE). To play up the gift angle, the page is "wrapped" with two pieces of twill ribbon. The "gift tag" is stamped with a compasslike image, and tied to the twill using fibers and an eyelet.

pretty titles to your scrapbook pages.
design element that also reinforces your topic.

Leeza's idea starters

Expand your horizons and think broadly when you brainstorm your travel-themed scrapbook pages.

(1) Where have you visited? Think big and small, not just about the splashy once-a-year planned vacations. Do you love going to the water park? Is there a quiet park where you like to eat lunch? Or a hot dog stand you always visit in a certain city?

(2) Describe an exotic meal you ate.

(3) What happened the first time you tried to speak a foreign language with a local?

(4) What is your favorite place you've been? What destination was most disappointing?

(5) What do you love about travel? What are your least favorite aspects of traveling?

(6) Who is your ideal traveling companion? Describe your dream trip.

(7) What kind of a traveler are you? Do you plan everything to the smallest detail, or are you a play-it-by-ear person?

(8) Are you good with directions or do you always get lost? How would you rather travel: by car, by plane, by boat, or by train?

(9) Do you love crowds? The beach? Hot weather or cold weather?

(10) If you were having overseas visitors, where would you take them in the United States?

Historical preservation

Scrapbooking can preserve memories for generations. To make that possible, you'll need to use acid-free materials that will minimize the fading and other damage to photographs and memorabilia. Get familiar with these archival products to make scrapbooks that will last.

PAPERS. Make sure every paper you use is acid- and lignin-free. This includes the papers that you use to print from your home computer.

INK. Every ink you use should be permanent and acid-free and shouldn't fade or run if it gets wet. If in doubt, test ink by using it on a piece of paper, sprinkling water on it, and setting the paper in bright sun for a few days.

ADHESIVES. All adhesives should be acid-, lignin-, and PVC-free. Beware of glue sticks and other adhesives that are easy to use but could yellow, crack, or damage photos over time.

STICKERS. Although there are thousands of stickers on the market, not all of them are acid-free. Look in crafts stores for those that are made especially for scrapbooking and are labeled acid- and lignin-free.

PAGE PROTECTORS. These plastic protectors prevent your photos and journaling from being smudged, torn, or damaged. Look for protectors that slip on from the side so dust can't settle down into the pages when the album is standing on a shelf. The plastic should be free of PVC, a gas-emitting chemical that can damage photographs.

PHOTO SLEEVES. If you want to incorporate memorabilia into your scrapbook—a child's birthday hat, a brochure of a day cruise from your honeymoon—invest in archival-quality plastic sleeves that can be inserted into the scrapbook. Place the item in the sleeve to keep any acids from migrating to other items on the page.

Tell me about...
your firsts

Living in Southern California, I often take for granted that I can dip my toes into the Pacific Ocean whenever the mood strikes and just sit on the sand and listen to the surf. I finally began to treasure those moments after I hosted a television show on "firsts." We arranged for a woman to see the ocean for the first time. She was spellbound. I put an infant into the arms of a grandmother, surprising her by telling her that it was her granddaughter. She had never met the child before and was holding the baby for the first time.

There is power in that single moment when something happens for the first time. I never feel more alive than in those moments, such as my first jump from an airplane in Texas, my first time hang gliding off the cliffs in Rio de Janeiro, and racing in my first Grand Prix in Long Beach, California. (Of course, I didn't go as fast in my own car as I did as a passenger in Tom Cruise's car!) Or getting my first kitty cat, a stray that my husband and kids rescued from the animal shelter and gave to me as a surprise.

When I was given a star on the fabled Hollywood Walk of Fame—now that was a first!—it was surreal. It wasn't even a question whether this would make it into my scrapbook. It was unbelievable to me that Dick Clark, who is one of my mentors, spoke at my star ceremony. I grew up in a small town in South Carolina, and I can hardly believe that life has taken me from The Land of Grits to The Land of Glitz. Those 3,000 miles between Hollywood and Dixie

I don't know about you, but I often find myself overwhelmed by all the items on my daily to-do list. It's easy to get caught up in that spiraling feeling of "How am I going to do all this?" That's why my scrapbooking mantra is, "Keep it simple." After all, scrapbooking should bring joy to your life, not more stress.

represent much more than physical distance. When I first got a job as a reporter on "Entertainment Tonight" in the early 1980s, I must have looked like a country bumpkin—the producers sent me to a makeup and wardrobe specialist. I wore glow-in-the-dark lipstick and had four-story hair. Hey, the bigger the hair, the closer to God, is what Naomi Judd always said. I laugh when I look at the photo of me with Bette Midler (LEFT)! I remember driving to work that day thinking, "I'm looking *gooood*!"

Just a glimpse into my diary of on-the-job experiences shows that I have had extraordinary privilege and access. I treasure every moment of my celebrity encounters, and now I have to smile when people call me a star. I mean, grateful as I am, can 25 years of telling the stories of the stars really make me a star? I call it the 'halo effect,' and I've enjoyed the residual glory. Mom always said, "It's a poor frog that doesn't praise his own pond," so I'm thrilled.

Scrapbook all your milestones, big and small: first paychecks, blind dates, the first time you stood up to your father. Stop and let those moments sink in. They are worth a couple of trips around the block in your brain. I'll bet you find they empower you, humble you, or awaken you.

HOLLYWOOD WALK OF FAME STAR CEREMONY. I took some low-tech shortcuts to create this filmstrip effect. I found actual 35-millimeter film and cut off the edges. Then I sized my photos into small squares and mounted them on black card stock. I added the film strips on both sides, backing it with narrow strips of white paper so the film edges show through.

1. Barry Manilow, 2003
2. Dolly Parton, 1988
3. George Burns, 1985
4. Steven Spielberg 1989
5. Arnold Schwarzenegger, 1988
6. Paul McCartney, 1989
7. Bette Midler, 1986
8. Jerry Lewis, 1993
9. Jamie Lee Curtis 2000
10. Kirk Douglas, 2001

Nate's Balloon Ride

2004

Nathan is my little baby, my last born and the one I have coddled the most. So it's tough to let go. At kindergarten graduation I lost it just thinking ahead to the day when his little felt mortarboard will give way to a real cap and gown. But that was nothing compared to watching him go up in his father's Parabounce balloon.

See, my husband, Steve, is a wonderfully eccentric, creative type who designed these one-man helium balloons which lift off the ground under your own power. We are often the test monkeys for the balloons. One day, when Steve had the balloons set up in our front yard, he decided it was time for Nathan to go up himself for the first time. Every cell in my body went haywire. My mothering instincts told me to keep this kid's feet firmly planted on the ground. I feigned a smile while Steve buckled him in. Nate glided up with squeals of delight. "Look at me, Mommy," he yelled. "I can see the tops of the trees!"

The experience was packed with symbolism. I saw my boy literally soar and begin to fly away from me. I couldn't protect him, couldn't stop him—and there was no room for me beside him. Puhleez, I was like a faucet of hot and cold running tears. My husband says I was just hormonal. Maybe that's why I wanted to smack Steve for suggesting that!

Five ways to scrapbook with friends

(1) Invite friends to bring all their old photos to your house, and spend the afternoon sorting and organizing.

(2) Hold a photo-cropping party; ask your guests to bring their favorite cropping tools.

(3) Have an embellishment swap: Everyone brings items they no longer want, such as frames, tags, and beads, and takes others home for free.

(4) Plan an idea exchange. Invite friends to bring their completed albums and share their favorite pages.

(5) Schedule a monthly crop for you and your friends. Ask them to bring along their can't-live-without-'em tools and supplies.

NATE'S BALLOON RIDE. Up, up, and away! When using papers with a strong pattern, such as this large yellow-and-purple floral, be sure to balance them with solid colors so they don't overwhelm the photos. Used sparingly as a page border and photo mat, the pattern works beautifully. The computer font used to print the title conveys the childlike excitement of the event. Feeling constrained by your fonts? Search the Internet, where you'll find options to match every mood and every layout. Some must be purchased, but many are free.

MORE INSPIRATION Plain blue paper is transformed to look like rippling water hitting the lake's edge for this FISH WISH layout that documents the first time two sisters went fishing. It's simple: Crumple up solid-blue paper, tear its edges, then lightly rub the surface with brown ink and blue chalk. To add a bit of whimsy to the title, which was stamped using dusty blue ink, uppercase and lowercase letters are mixed in the same word. Seven fishing flies hooked the imagination of this scrapbooker, who adhered them to the page.

The labels on the flies read:
BLUE GNAT
GRAY PEACOCK
BUCKTAIL CADDIS
CALIF MOSQUITO
BLUE UPRIGHT
BUCKTAIL COACHMAN

Kraig and I both grew up spending fun hours fishing with our fathers and we couldn't wait until our own children were old enough to learn how to fish from them too. Unfortunately, Papa Moore passed away before he got a chance to share his favorite hobby with them, but Grandpa Bergmann was more than willing to introduce Kaitlyn and Ashley to his love of fishing! When he and Grandma came to visit us in California, he brought the girls a perfect child-sized rod and a tackle box full of all sorts of fishy gizmos and flies he had tied himself. They were absolutely delighted with his gifts and couldn't wait to learn how to catch fish the same way he had taught their Daddy! Although they both became "expert" casters after just a few lessons, they never caught any fish, but still had a great time exploring the tackle box and spending this special time with their Grandpa. We all hope there will be many more fishing excursions together for many more years to come (and hopefully, a fish or two!) July 4, 2001

PEDAL POWER

Ashley was so excited when we told her she had outgrown her first bike and needed a bigger one. She fell in love with this blue & purple beauty (her two favorite colors!) and declared she was also ready to ditch her training wheels and learn to ride like the "big girls." It was frustrating at first, but she kept trying until she could ride like a pro! 10/5/03

MORE INSPIRATION It's a rite of passage that's perfect for the scrapbook: a youngster's first two-wheeler. For an interesting photo element on PEDAL POWER that appears to race across the page, six close-up shots of the bike were scanned into the computer, printed small (about 2"×1½"), and then butted together. As you plan a page, you may want to take photos specifically to fulfill a certain design function. This scrapbooker didn't have shots of the bike on hand; she shot them just for this page. The title was created using die-cut letters from the crafts store; the letters were stamped with a screen-pattern texture. A silver brad in the middle of a round tag makes the "o" look like a bike wheel. The secret to such straight journaling? Use a ruler to lightly pencil in guidelines; erase them after you finish writing.

Our 1st Anniversary
December 12, 1987

Our first year passed so quickly—it seems like only yesterday that we "tied the knot" and looked eagerly towards the future together! Kraig is still finishing his last year of college, so we didn't have much money to spend on gifts for each other, but Kraig surprised me with a heartfelt gift that was worth more than anything he could have spent on me! He gave me a cute tin full of 365 lovingly handwritten notes, and each one had a compliment, special favor, or treat written just for me. I got to pull one out for every day of the coming year and each one was wonderful to read and it gave me 365 more reasons to prove that I have the most wonderful husband in the world!

MORE INSPIRATION To commemorate a FIRST ANNIVERSARY—which occurred 17 years before this page was created—the scrapbooker gave this classic color-blocking layout an aged look. Just rough up the edges of the papers with sandpaper before adhering them to the page. Three vellum envelopes hold little handwritten notes. Vellum is a versatile material because it mutes and softens the colors and patterns of the papers underneath. Oops! Did you make a mistake? Disguise it with a ribbon, a beaded accent, even a small box of journaling.

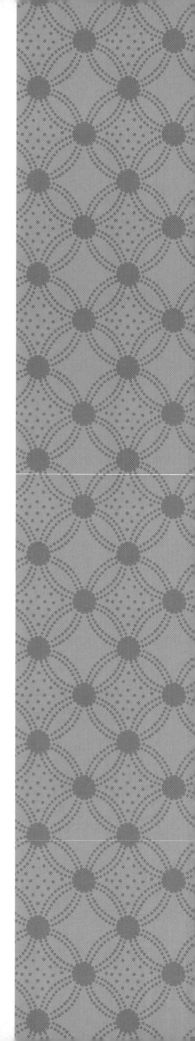

Leeza's idea starters

To jump-start the pages that document the "firsts" in your or your family's life, consider these ideas.

(1) First job.

(2) First kiss.

(3) What was the first formal dance you attended? What about the first Halloween costume party? Can you remember the first surprise party you attended? Were you the guest of honor?

(4) The day you found out you were pregnant.

(5) The first professional sports game you attended.

(6) The first "famous" person you met.

(7) Childhood is full of firsts. Do you remember your first visit from the Tooth Fairy? Your first bike? Your first toy? What about your first black eye?

(8) Do you remember your first haircut? What about the first perm you got?

(9) Describe your first apartment and the first house you bought.

(10) What was the first meal you cooked for your partner? Where did you have your first date?

(11) What was the first meal you burned?

(12) When did you take your first airplane trip?

Embellishments

Little flourishes are one of the design elements that differentiate a scrapbook from a mere photo album. Check your local crafts store for an almost endless array of embellishments, including these popular items.

PUNCHES. Special punches are used to cut out paper shapes and to trim corners of photos in rounded or decorative shapes.

DIE CUTS. These precut paper pieces come in all sorts of shapes, including letters and numbers. Buy the die cuts already made, or invest in your own equipment and cut a host of designs yourself.

STICKERS. Stickers are often grouped in packs according to a theme, such as the outdoors, babies, or weddings. Alphabet and number stickers are available too. Be sure to buy only acid-free stickers so they won't damage other elements on the page.

STAMPS. Many types are available, including alphabets, border designs, photo frames, quotes, and motifs related to a particular theme. When stamping, be sure to use ink that won't smear or fade; if in doubt, test it before using it on your scrapbook page.

MORE, MORE, MORE! The list of embellishments that you can buy at your local crafts store is infinite: metal frames, paper tags and flowers, beaded designs, tiny envelopes, ribbons, twine, embroidery floss, and on and on.

FOUND OBJECTS. Many of the embellishments you'll want to include are things you'll pick up during your travels: ticket stubs, postcards, foreign currency (it's colorful and exotic), seashells, locks of hair, baby announcements, church bulletins, party invitations, and menus. Any of these will make a one-of-a-kind addition to your pages. However, only use items that you know are acid-free.

Take time to ...
share with others

When my siblings and I decided to have a party for my parents' 50th wedding anniversary, it was more than a little bittersweet. After all, we had always thought Mom and Dad would take center stage and show off their dance moves as the "Tennessee Waltz"

played. But a few years shy of the date, my mom's life story was rewritten by Alzheimer's disease, and my dad's dance partner was now a bent-over woman with a shuffling step and a worried expression. Still, they had made it to this milestone, so celebrate we did. We hired a band and had dinner at a local restaurant. Since Mom wouldn't be able to attend, we dropped by the facility where she lived and had a private celebration with just Dad and us kids.

That's when my sweet, talented sister, Cammy, unveiled what she had been working on for weeks: a scrapbook of my parents' lives together (BELOW). It was all there, from their engagement to Dad's days in the Army to their three kids. Old neighbors and good friends wrote letters and sent mementos of a life well spent. My dad wept when he opened it. He took it with him every day to his antiques store and shared his stories with customers, whether they were interested or not. I've never seen anything get such a reaction from this man, but somewhere in the pages of this "Carlos and Jean" scrapbook was a comforting reminder of who he was, the people he loved, and the places he went. Memories matter.

The first scrapbook I received as a gift was in 1986 from the organizers of the March of Dimes telethon. It includes pictures, letters, and highlights of the broadcast as well as shots of my tour through pediatric hospital wards. I love to look at the hairstyles, the dresses (one made me look just like Big Bird!),

If you're looking for the most meaningful way to punctuate the time you've spent with someone or the most intimate way to honor a loved one's hobby, trip, or passion, make a scrapbook for him or her. It is a way to share and celebrate like no other.

and the people who meant so much to me. I also received scrapbooks following my bridal shower and the ceremony when I got my star on the Hollywood Walk of Fame. These gifts become increasingly more valuable over time. Having someone else bear witness to our lives keeps us anchored in the belief that we matter.

Of course, I've also made and given away many scrapbooks as gifts. Buying presents is great, but investing the time to make something special like a scrapbook is real love in action. The pictures don't have to be professional and the words don't have to be perfect, but the recipient of the gift will think they are.

Last summer I made a scrapbook for Oprah Winfrey. She had invited me to come on her show to talk about Alzheimer's disease and share my work with The Leeza Gibbons Memory Foundation. This was big stuff. How could I thank her? I focused on her passion and dedication to the people of South Africa. I made her a scrapbook about her recent trip to that country, and I used her own words and pictures. She noticed every detail, every embellishment, every frame. She told me she loved reliving the stories of something so deeply personal. How cool.

The lesson is obvious. When you don't know what to give someone, hold up a mirror to his or her life. Find the thing that stirs the soul of the person you want to honor; that's what your scrapbook should be about. Everyone finds value in reflecting on the places they've gone and the lives they've touched. It's a soulprint that comes beautifully alive in a scrapbook.

One of my favorite gifts (ABOVE) was a scrapbook from my son Nathan's day-care teachers. They lovingly detailed everything from his favorite book and his favorite outfit during dress up (red cowboy boots and a fringed vest) to his personality quirks and his best buddies.

FIFTY YEARS. I will never forget the powerful moment when my father saw his life celebrated, honored, and archived in this scrapbook, which my sister, Cammy, put together. It was the perfect anniversary gift.

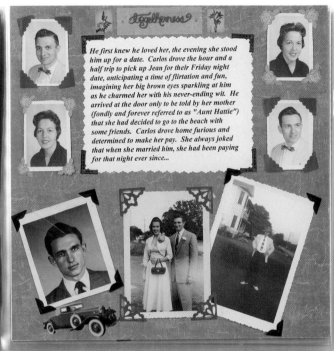

He first knew he loved her, the evening she stood him up for a date. Carlos drove the hour and a half trip to pick up Jean for their Friday night date, anticipating a time of flirtation and fun, imagining her big brown eyes sparkling at him as he charmed her with his never-ending wit. He arrived at the door only to be told by her mother (fondly and forever referred to as "Aunt Hattie") that she had decided to go to the beach with some friends. Carlos drove home furious and determined to make her pay. She always joked that when she married him, she had been paying for that night ever since...

After serving at Ft. Jackson from December 1950 until January 1952, Carlos left the army life for family life.

Leeza's idea starters

A gift of a homemade scrapbook is a way to honor
and celebrate a person like no other gift can. It's an
especially great idea for the person who seems to have
everything or is impossible to buy for. Best of all,
a scrapbook is one-size-fits-all. Get started with
these ideas.

(1) Almost any occasion is an appropriate one to
give a scrapbook: weddings, birthdays, anniversaries,
graduations from high school or college, bridal
showers, baby showers, going-away parties, Mother's
Day, and Father's Day.

(2) A small 5"×7" or 7"×7" book is ideal for a gift
scrapbook because it's easy to fill, which makes the
process less intimidating. Narrow topics work best.
Consider a book of inspirational quotes with personal
snapshots or a series of wishes for a birthday girl.

(3) Give scrapbooks to commemorate difficult events
too, like the death of a beloved pet or the rebirth of a
house after a devastating fire. A "celebration of life"
memory book will be appreciated by the family of
someone who has passed away.

(4) Need an end-of-the-year gift for a teacher? Put
your child to work creating a scrapbook.

(5) If you are a teacher, coach, or day-care provider—
or anyone else who spends time with kids—consider
putting together a scrapbook to share with a child's
parents and relatives. Special friends, aunts, and
grandmoms are great sources of stories and moments
that give a new perspective to a child's journey.

Storing and caring

Protect your beautiful scrapbook pages and treasured photos from wear and tear with these tips.

ALBUMS. These books or binders will hold your scrapbook pages. The album you choose will guide many of the decisions you make as you scrapbook, so ask yourself these questions before you start.

▪ Will this album stand alone, or will it be one of a series? If you're planning a series (for instance, a book for each of your children), choose an album size and cover (they come in leather, fabric, etc.) that you'll want to repeat for each book.

▪ How many elements do you want to include on a page? If the book will be filled only with photos, a smaller album might do. But if you plan to include journaling and embellishments, you'll need a bigger album. Popular sizes for albums are 7"×7", 8"×10", 8½"×11", 12"×12" and 12"×15". (All the scrapbook pages you see in this book are 12"×12" and fit perfectly in a 12"×12" album.)

▪ Will you want to add pages later? If so, select a scrapbook that is expandable.

▪ Do you want to create two-page layouts? If so, you'll need an album that lies flat when you open it, such as a post-bound or strap-style album.

PAGE PROTECTORS AND SLEEVES. Plastic page protectors, which slip over finished pages, help prevent smudges, tears, and other damage. Not every album comes with page protectors as an option; choose one that does. Plastic sleeves can be inserted in a scrapbook to hold nonacid-free memorabilia, such as old letters or newspaper clippings. Like page protectors, they should be free of PVC, a gas-emitting chemical that can damage photographs.

PHOTO BOXES. Store your yet-to-be-used photographs in acid-free photo boxes, organizing them by general categories. Keep negatives in a separate place so that if your scrapbook or photo boxes are lost or damaged, you can reprint the photos. Also, store digital photos on CDs so you can reprint them if needed.

glossary

ACID-FREE. Identifies scrapbooking products that are safe to use with your photographs. Why is this so important? Photographs have acid in them from processing. When those acids come in contact with other acidic products (such as some papers, adhesives, and embellishments), a chemical reaction will occur that can eventually cause discoloration and damage.

ADHESIVE. A substance such as glue or tape that can be used to adhere two or more scrapbook elements to each other.

ALBUM. A book or binder in which scrapbook pages can be stored and organized.

ARCHIVAL-QUALITY OR ARCHIVAL-SAFE. Indicates that a scrapbooking product is safe to use with photographs and will help preserve the pages long-term. These terms may be used interchangeably with acid-free.

BORDER. A decorative band that runs along the edge of something, such as a scrapbook page or a photo mat.

BUFFERED PAPER. Paper that's been treated with an alkaline substance to make it acid-free.

CARD STOCK. A heavy weight paper that works well for scrapbooking.

CHALKING. A technique for adding subtle color and dimension to a scrapbook page by applying chalk, which can be purchased at a scrapbooking store. Chalk can be applied to a page with a variety of applicators, including cotton swabs and eye-makeup sponges.

COLORFAST. A pigment or dye that resists fading or running under normal conditions.

CRAFTS KNIFE. An indispensable tool for cutting. It's metal and has disposable blades.

CROPPING. Changing a photograph by physically cutting it or manipulating it with a computer.

DIE CUT. A shaped piece of paper that has been cut with a special punching blade called a die.

EMBELLISHMENTS. Decorative enhancements for your scrapbook pages, such as ribbons, buttons, and metal photo corners.

INK-JET PRINTING. A type of computer printing that uses a small head to spray ink onto paper.

JOURNALING. A term used to describe the writing on scrapbook pages.

LABEL. A small space to write a photo caption, date, or name, and often made of paper, ribbons, or tags.

LAYOUT. The design formed by all the elements on a scrapbook page.

LASER PRINTING. A type of computer printing similar to the dry process of a photocopier.

MAT. A decorative paper that's adhered to the back of a photo and frames or borders the photo. Use one paper or several layers to create an interesting accent.

ORGANIZATIONAL BAG. A carrying case designed to store scrapbooking supplies.

PALETTE. The range of colors used on a particular scrapbook page or series of pages.

PENS AND PENCILS. Indispensable tools for journaling and measuring.

PHOTO CORNERS. An embellishment for framing or a tool for mounting photos. Look for versions made of paper, metal, ribbons, and other materials.

SCORE. To mark with lines, scratches, or notches to aid in folding papers.

SCRAPBOOK. A book composed of many scrapbook pages.

STAMPING PADS AND INK. Use these tools (available at crafts and scrapbooking stores) to add depth, color, and intensity to the edges of scrapbooking papers.

VELLUM. A lightweight transparent paper that's a favorite of scrapbookers. Available in a range of colors and patterns.

index

I hope you've enjoyed *Scrapbooking Traditions* and that you're ready to embark on a lifetime journey with scrapbooking. Scrapbooking is such an important part of my life that I've partnered with Xyron to create Leeza Gibbons Legacies ®, my new scrapbooking and paper-crafting collection. All of the patterned papers that were used to create the scrapbook pages in this book are from my collection. I'm so proud of this collection that I wanted to share it with you. You'll find 16 sample paper designs on the following pages. They're ready to tear out and become a source of inspiration for your own pages and stories. After all, there's no better time to start scrapbooking than right now. Just remember, memories matter.

Leeza

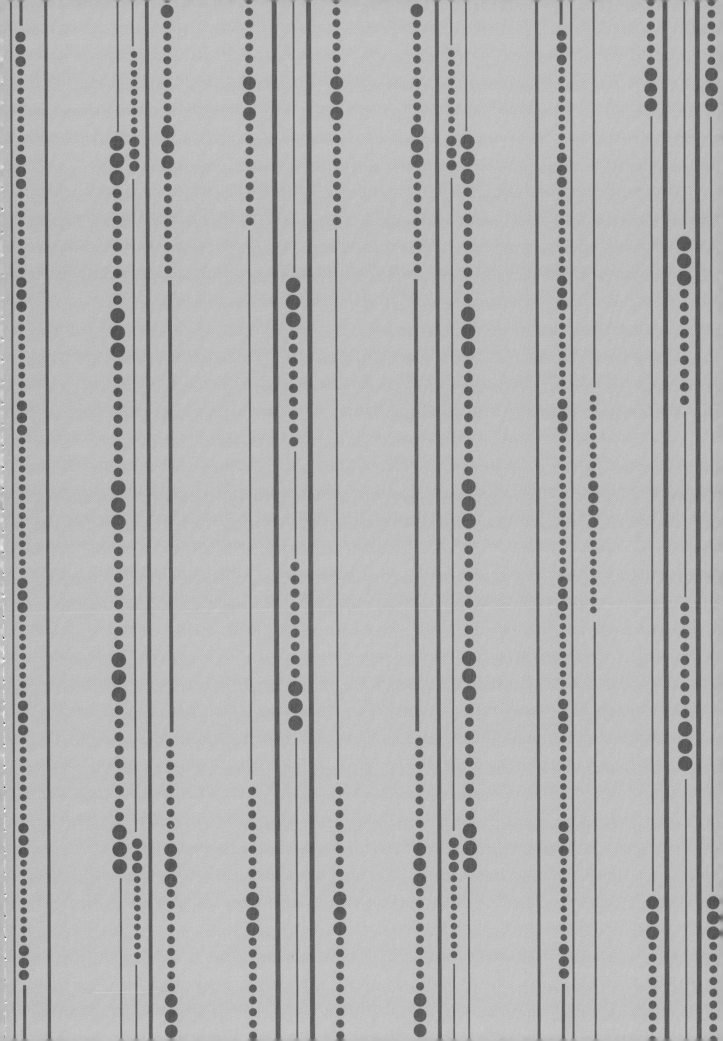

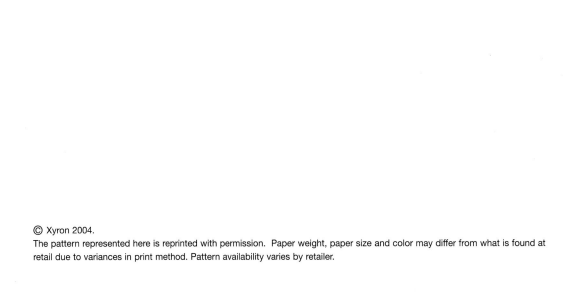